ONE MAN'S T

ONE MAN'S TESTIMONY

NORMAN GOODALL

SCM PRESS LTD

British Library Cataloguing in Publication Data

Goodall, Norman
    One man's testimony.—2nd ed.
    1. Christian life
    I. Title
    248.4   BV4501.2

    ISBN 0–334–02237–1

334 02237 1

First published 1949
by Independent Press Ltd
This reissue published 1985
by SCM Press Ltd
26–30 Tottenham Road, London N1

Printed in Great Britain by
Richard Clay (The Chaucer Press) Ltd
Bungay, Suffolk

FOR MY FRIENDS

CONTENTS

Memoir

'Good wine needs no bush' must be among the most abused of quotations. Constantly it is introduced in order to be ignored, or contradicted. If applied to this enterprise of writing some kind of preface or introduction to the reissue of Norman Goodall's *One Man's Testimony* it certainly invites the question why the book should not stand on its own. It has proved its permanent value by the call for its reissue thirty-six years after it first appeared. More than this, since it is a personal testimony, and contains much material that is modestly and even deliciously autobiographical, it can be expected that the reader will soon know what manner of man the author was.

The excuse for what I now write is to be found in two things. One is the modesty to which I have just referred. Another pen must reveal something of the stature and achievements of the author. Yet again, Norman Goodall lived for three and a half decades after he wrote this book. Those who have not known him personally, and perhaps most of all a younger generation that has arisen since his major achievements, may wish to know something more of his life. Quite simply it can only be expected that those who encounter the beguiling personality revealed in this book will want to know what happened afterwards. He was eighty-eight when he died, but, although the last two or three years were a time of increasing physical frailty, until that point he had been active in many things of singular ecumenical value. To his very last days he remained what he had always been – a loved father in God to many.

Perhaps the most striking tribute to Norman Goodall came from a friend who had been his resolute opponent in the largest task he ever undertook, which was the integration of the International Missionary Council with the World Council of Churches. He had been the secretary of the joint committee of the two bodies which was appointed in 1955 to bring the integration about. In 1961 it was triumphantly achieved at the Third Assembly of the World Council held at New Delhi in 1961. The speed and eventual smoothness with which this came about may rightly be regarded as the largest achievement of Norman Goodall's outward life. He was used by God to bring into being the present shape of the world-wide ecumenical instrument. Not all, however, rejoiced in this. Within the World Council there had been notable opposition to the incorporation of a missionary element in that Council from the Orthodox Churches. Many of them saw missionary work as represented by Protestant evangelical groups 'evangelizing' lands of Orthodox tradition. On the IMC side, too, there were resolute opponents who feared blunting of the purpose to go out to all the world with the saving word of the gospel by making it only part – and possibly a disregarded part – of the whole range of activities to which the World Council of Churches gave rise.

Perhaps chief among the missionary opponents of integration was the redoubtable general secretary of the Church Missionary Society, Canon 'Max' Warren. Warren was one of the leading missionary statesmen of the world, a man of immense influence in the life of the younger churches, who read phenomenally widely and reflected deeply on the issues that confront church and society today. The action of such a man in choosing, when writing his memoirs *Crowded Canvas* (Hodder 1974), to make of Norman Goodall the luminous exemplar of all that was best in the ecumenical movement is remarkable testimony of the effect of his personality and spirit. After writing of Norman's unusual gifts of speech Max Warren goes on:

> Norman has other great qualities, not least that of a generous understanding of the views of other people, and a deep respect for personality, which he recognises as being itself part of every situation, every problem, every viewpoint. This has made him an ideal negotiator. He is no bulldozer, as have been not a few who have played a leading part in the Ecumenical Movement. In the acute tensions which have sometimes been generated between North Americans and those from the continent of Europe, he has played the mediating role of the British to perfection, with a foot affectionately placed in both camps. It is to the world's infinite loss that there has been no comparable British figure in the political field in the last twenty years.

The weight of the judgment expressed in that last sentence deserves pondering, coming from the source that it does. The tribute closed with this sentence: 'And if he reads these words I hope he will forgive me, for ... I am expressing not only affection and admiration for an individual, but a lively devotion to all that is best and truest in the Ecumenical Movement.'

Norman Goodall's direct service of that movement had begun in 1944, just five years before the original publication of *One Man's Testimony*. He had been recruited from the staff of the London Missionary Society to be one of the secretaries of the International Missionary Council. He was perhaps unusual in that generation of full-time servants of the ecumenical movement in being nurtured not by prior service in, say, the World Student Christian Federation or the YMCA, but by being a minister in local churches (in Walthamstow and New Barnet).

The International Missionary Council was the first fruits of the World Missionary Conference held at Edinburgh in 1910, which is usually seen as the starting-point of modern ecumenism. Its structure perhaps showed something of the caution that surrounded a first attempt to create an international Christian instrument. There were secretaries in both London and New York, and only later was a general secretary appointed. What is understood to have been a policy decision at that point to avoid difficulty by not appointing an existing secretary to the new office led to Goodall being passed over. It was an amazing decision in the light of the gifts he had shown. He accepted it with characteristic humility and grace. But there can be no doubt that it hurt. In a measure, too, it was frustrating, for it prevented him from bringing the full contribution his gifts equipped him to bring to the final phase of the life of the IMC as a separate body.

Nevertheless, his appointment to full-time ecumenical service in 1944 meant that he was able to give a full quarter of a century of service to the movement. He gave it in a variety of offices. Perhaps the fact that, apart from a concluding two years at Geneva as Assistant General Secretary of the World Council, his ecumenical service was always based in Britain gave it some of its special quality. That quality resided in the fact that his profound commitment to all that was ecumenical, emphatically embracing both the unity and missionary dimensions of that word, was rooted in an equally deep loyalty to his own Congregational tradition with its belief in the gathered church, the little flock of Christ covenanted together by grace.

In that tradition he held all the honorary offices that

were open to him. In 1955–56 he was Chairman of the Congregational Union of England and Wales (as it then was), delivering from the chair an address of such insight and power that it would repay republication thirty years later. From 1962 to 1968 he was Moderator of the International Congregational Council. The Free Churches of England and Wales honoured him by the Moderatorship of the Free Church Federal Council for 1966–67. When the United Reformed Church, uniting his own church with the Presbyterian Church of England, came into being in 1972 he rejoiced that his own tradition had been to the fore in breaking the barrier which seems to inhibit trans-confessional unions in these islands. Certainly there were leaders in the newly united church who would have wished to call him to the moderatorship had it not been thought too great a burden to load on to a man in his late seventies. There was clear awareness that the church had no more distinguished member of its ministry.

These offices, however, were but outward recognition of a commitment to a form of churchmanship which had nourished and sustained his own life. His ecumenical service brought him thankful understanding of many other traditions, and he gratefully acknowledged the enrichment that had come to him through the range of ecclesiastical experience and history which his service opened to him. He was nevertheless never tempted towards a rootless ecumenism that nourishes a half-concealed contempt for the little companies of Christians over-housed in rows of pitch-pine pews who are nonetheless trying to offer Christ their loyalty and obedience in perhaps rather humdrum situations. They might be 'not many wise, not many mighty', but this man, emphatically unusually wise and mighty in his powers of mind and spirit, saw them as companies of grace to whom God in the wonder of his self-giving would reveal his will if only they waited on him.

He rejoiced in the freedom of his own tradition of churchmanship. He saw it as a freedom given and controlled by grace. It was never to be mistaken for a moment for individualistic license. He certainly believed in the truth of Paul's words, 'and where the Spirit of the Lord is, there is liberty', but he would never have misused those words to suggest that order has no place in the life of the church. The order was a gift of the Spirit of the Lord.

His was a catholic churchmanship that grew and grew in appreciation of the great range of Christian tradition that he served through the ecumenical instruments. But it was never either an ethereal churchmanship, unrelated to the actualities of our human condition, or a radical churchmanship which despised the conservatism of the little church on the corner.

The catholicity of his churchmanship was illustrated by two major tasks which he fulfilled in the closing years of his life. They were tasks at opposite ends of the ecclesiastical spectrum, but the two brought him equal delight. One was his chairmanship of the demanding conversations between the United Reformed Church and the Churches of Christ (Disciples). They were demanding because they had to face a major theological issue: how can the convictions of churches believing only in believer's baptism and of a church believing and practising infant baptism be reconciled without doctrinal fudging? It was also a task which had to face a measure of resistance from some URC ministers. Why, so early in their own experience of union, should they have to face radical adjustments to accommodate a quite small denomination? Norman Goodall was superbly equipped by conviction and experience to defuse that kind of opposition. He was able to rejoice at the uniting assembly which saw again two hitherto divided churches become one.

The other task related to the largest of the Christian churches – the Roman Catholic. When in his mid-seventies Norman was invited to lecture on the ecumenical movement at the Pontifical Gregorian University in Rome. In one sense it was a natural invitation. Apart from the wealth of his ecumenical experience, he had written in 1961 *The Ecumenical Movement*, published by Oxford University Press. This was a balanced and clear survey of ecumenical developments, brought up to date ten years later by *Ecumenical Progress*, sub-titled 'A Decade of Change in the Ecumenical Movement 1961–71'. In another sense it was an unusual invitation, for it was extended to one whose churchmanship would seem to be far removed from that of the Vatican.

The experiment was a triumphant success. Norman Goodall was invited to make his base in Rome at the English College, whose Rector then was Monsignor Cormac Murphy O'Connor, now Bishop of Arundel and Brighton. Bishop Cormac gave an address at the service of thanksgiving for Norman's life. He described the relationship between this senior guest from a Protestant communion and the young students. 'They found him the easiest person to talk to, for he had a marvellous facility for entering into their interests and their concerns, and yet one should remember that he was nearly eighty years old, and they for their part in their early twenties.'

In one passage in his tribute Bishop Cormac penetrated to one of the most wonderful aspects of Norman's personality.

The gifts of God have a certain lightness and grace about them which a corresponding delicacy and balance in the receiver achieved through an asceticism or expectation. It is sometimes called 'watching in prayer'. Norman Goodall had the quality of always being open, expectant, waiting on the inspiration of the Holy Spirit, not only for the Church, but for all during his long life. His graciousness was a kind of hope, a hope that does not reject the past, does not see only the darkness, the failures, the hopes unfulfilled, the vanity of human wishes. This kind of hope does not overlook these things, but it sees them in the light of a forgiving and transforming power, that same power from which I have received my being and towards which each of us is travelling in the light of hope; it is full of thankfulness and of that special graciousness that is called gratitude. Norman had that kind of ripeness and trust in the providence of God, and it was good to meet it and to recognize it.

Much of what has been written up to now has been about the offices and achievements of the author of the book that follows. The quotation which I have just given from Bishop Cormac, who became a friend of Norman's old age and sustained that friendship to the last days of his life, takes us to the man himself, who was far more important than his outward career. Indeed his service of the ecumenical movement was a direct expression of a personality so infused by the grace of God that he brought graciousness to every human contact, and therefore was rarely equipped for what is fundamentally a work of reconciliation. There are some men whose achievements sound like a great roll of drums, but whose personalities are as hollow as the drums that would sound it. There are others, and Norman was emphatically one of them, whose outward work *is* in fact a working out of the deep convictions that they cherish, and whose inner quality far exceeds the external record.

There is, however, one apparently external thing which

was so much part of Norman Goodall that it must be stressed even in a brief pen-portrait of him. He possessed a well-nigh incredible gift of words, not only in writing – of which this book provides clear evidence – but in speech. Even unprepared speeches, made in the pressure of debate and in response to questions which had just arisen, were marked by a flow of perfectly balanced sentences, mellifluous in their flow and with every word seeming the precisely accurate word to convey his meaning. So exceptional was the degree of his possession of this gift that no one could write of him without mentioning it. Thus Canon Max Warren, within the tribute already referred to, says, 'He could so spin words together, and lighten them with gentle humour, that one's critical faculties were lulled to sleep.' To Warren, Norman 'possessed a gift of language which made him one of the most fascinating speakers to whom to listen'. He added, 'I have heard many great orators, but none, I think, more persuasive than Norman.'

In fact, even though he was born in Victoria's day, there was nothing of the orotund orator at all about his phenomenal powers of speech. There were no rolling periods or flamboyant purple passages. He was really the Henry James of the pulpit and the council chamber. Words poured out, but there was never the slightest hint of verbosity. It was delight in words used with precision, and to express balanced thought. Language was always used with reverence for its beauty. The sentences and periods might have some of the complexity of Henry James (whose work he indeed loved) but meaning was always pellucidly clear. The complexity was necessary because integrity demanded the acknowledgment, at least in passing, of the other considerations and arguments that had to be weighed if an honest judgment were to be reached.

Although in some substantial degree this gift of speech

must have been a natural endowment, it was nourished by steeping himself from early in life to its very end in the best of our literature. It was also related to the immense hold on his life of beauty in so many of its forms. Like so many others he was perplexed by the relationship between beauty and goodness. He spoke of this in that remarkable address already referred to from the chair of the Congregational Union. 'I find the gulf between the aesthetic and the ethical one of the most humbling and frightening of all mysteries, believing – as I do – that beauty and goodness proceed from the same God, the one and only God.' (It is the theme, too, of a memorable passage of that which follows.) However great remained his perplexity about the relationship, his whole life proclaimed that there was one, and that it was intimate. The character of his speech therefore was not merely an external thing: it was sacramental of this man's faith. If he had to speak of that faith, or of the life of the church which enshrines it, it was natural for him to try to enshrine what he had to say, even when he had to speak spontaneously, in the beauty which he believed to be one of the attributes and manifestations of God.

There was one very significant and unexpected use to which he could put this winning power of speech. If his words could lull the critical faculty to sleep they also had a most valuable power to anaesthetize when a surgical operation had to be done. He was a wonderful surgeon upon our egotisms. Not a few have come to after some glorious cascade of balanced prose only to find that while under the anaesthetic an unpleasant bit of self-assertiveness or of repulsive ambition had been removed with little more than post-operative discomfort.

For Norman was in the full Christian sense a loving man. That remarkable missionary Amy Carmichael of

Dohnavur refers somewhere to 'the weak kind of sympathy which does not brace the one who receives it, but sends her away saying "How loving so-and-so is. She always understands me" '. Norman was never like that. Love was never sentimentality; his love for his friends was never weakening. He loved us as we were, but being the man in Christ that he was, he wanted us to be what by God's grace we could be. His love for us was therefore at one and the same time sustaining and bracing. He reflected his Master in this, that the sheer fact that he cared so much for all with whom he came into close contact conveyed its own challenge to be better men and women.

His own tradition knew nothing of the language of catholic spirituality in terms of spiritual directors and fathers in God, but those who knew Norman Goodall knew much of the reality of these things. He was spiritual guide and father in God to many who carried major responsibility in the life of the churches. It was natural for them to turn to him at points of decision in their lives, and for guidance and direction when they were going through a sticky patch. They were sure that they would find in him an unusual combination of loving austerity, abundant humanity and rare spiritual insight.

To think of him is naturally to think of joy and serenity, but it would be unwise to think of these as merely the gift of nature. They were the gifts of grace. He was a man who had faced long and deep frustrations in public and private life. His sensitivity and fastidiousness were such as to make him often raw to the impact of the crude and the ugly. He was in a real sense a vulnerable man who much needed the garrison of God's peace in a world which often bewildered him by its evil. More than this, because he was so sensitive, the ultimate questions of our life and destiny were questions with which he had to wrestle to the end.

He did not live by certainty, but by faith. It was a faith constantly renewed by his devotional life. The reader of what follows must not see it as the words of one who just happened to be a man naturally Christian. There was a struggle beneath the serenity. What he emphatically was was a man who knew where grace could be found, and how the gift could be renewed in the life of faith. Not only in the worship of the church and in private devotion was his sense of God's grace constantly nurtured, but in a multiplicity of human contacts with people of all ages which continued to his death. This man who seemed to have such remarkable inner resources, and could make himself free of great areas of music and literature, humbly confessed to the end of his days his dependence on the stimulus of other people. The cynical saying 'Hell is other people' would have seemed to him a blasphemy.

At the close of his long days he rejoiced with his wife, Doris, in the patriarchal and matriarchal status they had acquired as their three children's families grew by marriage and the coming of great-grandchildren. In the closing months of frailty he was lovingly cared for by an old and very dear friend, Dr Elizabeth Welford. Had he lived but two days longer they would have been joined in marriage in the chapel of Mansfield College, Oxford, a place which evoked Norman's deepest gratitude and loyalty. That was not to be, but it may be seen as symbolic of Norman's joy in how God's grace and love are reflected in our human relations that to his last hours he looked forward to that sealing of affection in worship.

What follows is in every sense 'One Man's Testimony'. The passing even of years which seem to have drastically eroded so many past certainties have left its central witness unimpaired, because it is not about the conventional faith of a generation but the living experience of a man who tried to live by authentic faith. The exploration of God's grace here described went on with zest and joy until he moved to that life in which we know even as also we are known.

Kenneth Slack

CHAPTER ONE

ACROSS TWO WARS

I CAME to manhood in a different universe from this
—or so it often seems. My youth lies at the other
side of two world wars. Between the atmosphere of
that time and the prevailing tone of things today
there are differences which an older generation may vainly
try to interpret to a younger. It is not—for example—
that wars were then unthinkable. One of my earliest childhood impressions is associated with the smell of an elder
brother's army clothes as he greeted me on his return
from the South African war. Between then and the end of
that other universe in 1914 I heard plenty of talk about the
possibility of further wars. The Balkans always seemed
about to go up in smoke, with dangerous consequences
for the rest of us. We were constantly being warned
against Germany; many of the political discussions to
which I listened at home gathered round the question
whether we ought to prepare faster for war than the
Liberal Government was apparently doing. Even the Far
East included a threat to our peace. Wasn't Japan, flushed
with the success of Port Arthur, a portent? Could white
and European dominance in world affairs be maintained
indefinitely without a struggle? And what would be the
consequences for Britain of such movements as that which,
not long since, had given birth to the Indian National
Congress? It has often been assumed in recent years, as
men have contrasted the present with the pre-1914 past,
that "the invasion of our private lives by the larger destinies of mankind"—to borrow a phrase from George

Eliot—is something that we older folk never knew in the placid beginning of this century. But I question the assumption. Our world was more restless than is commonly remembered and our private lives were constantly being invaded by the larger destinies of mankind. War was definitely not unthinkable.

Nor does the difference lie in the economic insecurity which frets the present generation. At least, this isn't a difference which, in my personal case, explains the contrast between the atmosphere of the two generations. My early home-life was far less cushioned by social securities than would be true of comparable homes today. I was one of a large family, heroically but precariously maintained by parents whose working week was nearer 90 than 40 hours.

The retail shop where we lived had been an escape for my father from factory labour unprotected by any form of unemployment insurance. But, very soon, over the fitful security and independence of our little shop there came the shadow of multiple-stores descending on the village and squeezing out the small trader. Brave and generous parents shielded the youngsters from anxiety but I knew why my first educational opportunity could not take me beyond the sixpence a week charged by the local "Higher Grade" School. The neighbouring Grammar School fees were out of the question and in any case it was taken for granted that I should start earning my keep at fourteen. I make these personal references only to illustrate the similarity rather than the contrast between some of the insecurities of my earlier environment and those of a later generation. In so far as contrasts exist, there are points at which these latter days show marked improvement. At any rate, a sense of life's precariousness, knowledge of the struggle to ward off want and cope with fear, cannot be claimed as the peculiar inheritance of a post-1914 or post-1939 generation.

When I reflect on much else that goes deeper than external events or prevailing circumstances, I find it still more difficult to account for the feeling that the universe in which I came to manhood's certainties was fundamentally different from that which my younger contemporaries know. Life hurt then as now. The "vile blows and buffets of the world" were not less likely to be felt. Loved ones died—often prematurely. Personal disloyalties and betrayals possessed their peculiar sting. Disappointment was bitter, frustration brought that numbing sense of defeat with resentment at the heart of it. Consciousness of failure, humiliating awareness of moral weakness and spiritual impotence went deep. At this point, in fact, my generation was probably capable of experiencing greater depths of personal humiliation than its successor. The word "sin" has less meaning now and is less frightening than it was. Personal responsibility for what goes wrong is not so readily accepted, and therefore self-condemnation and contrition are not so widely experienced. At its greatest depths, at the points where religious conviction has its most intimate significance, life was not less grave or heart-searching than it is today.

Does the difference lie at a more intellectual level? Is it that the "acids of modernity" have so affected the rational elements in belief that intellectual honesty and religious conviction are less compatible with one another than they appeared to be a few decades ago? This is commonly assumed to be a principal point of contrast between the atmosphere in which the older ones amongst us reached conviction and that in which a new generation seeks religious certainty. But again, the assumption is open to question. Of course, taking a longer view of the history of religious thought, there is undoubtedly an enormous difference between the intellectual climate of our time and that of the great ages of faith. Further, movements of thought which, thirty or forty years ago, were of fairly recent origin, have not only accelerated rapidly in the last few decades; their implications for faith have proved to be more radical than was at first recognized. The main contrast, however, which I am discussing at the moment lies within a much briefer span than the one which marks these major epochs in thought. To return to the personal story which I am using to illustrate my argument, the period in which I came to religious certainty was one in which the cold winds of scepticism, which have since gathered hurricane force, were already blowing powerfully, and the windows of my home were by no means closed to them. Ours was not a scholar's home, but in so far as intellectual movements and arguments touch the ordinary run of men's lives and influence, one way or another, their "will to believe," we knew to some extent which way the wind was blowing. Most of the publications of the Rationalist Press Association were read and discussed with avidity by my father. Cheap reprints of the works of the nineteenth-century agnostics were honoured and used in the family library. Father was always inclined to credit scientists with greater intellectual integrity than parsons and there were times when it was difficult to decide whether—convinced Methodist as he was—he admired John Wesley or Charles Bradlaugh most. Behind this domestic setting we knew that there existed the deep and growing scepticism of the Edwardian era and already there were signs that its corrosive influence was the more potent because it co-existed with much outward observance of religious conventions. I am by no means convinced that the present generation is more seriously exposed to rational arguments against faith than was my own.

Yet I return to my earlier admission that as I look back across two world wars I can understand why one of my generation may struggle in vain to interpret to post-1939 youth convictions reached in a pre-1914 existence. Wars were not unthinkable then, but now they have occurred, on such a scale and of such a character, the universe in which they happen—and may happen again—has clouds in its firmament more forbidding than we ever knew. Economic insecurity was real then, and at many points far more cruel in its consequences for the individual than it is today, yet both endurance and the will to overcome seemed more possible and more worthwhile than they have since become. As for the agnostics and sceptics of the last century and the early years of the present one, serious and formidable as were their assaults on faith, I think it was easier then to feel in one's bones that they were wrong, wherever the arguments lay; whereas I suspect that a new generation, assaulted by the newer unbelief, is more inclined to feel in its bones that the unbeliever is right, whatever may be the arguments of the clever but unintelligible theologians. Even in the attitude of the agnostics then, there was often a subtle quality, more of spirit than of logic, which belied their reasons and made it possible for the believer to feel that in converse with them deep was calling to deep. Nowadays the debate seems intellectually harsher and colder and the protagonists spiritually farther apart.

Whether, in face of these differences which go deeper than reason, such verbal testimony as I can offer in this book will speak conviction across a generation, I cannot say. I can only make my testimony and leave it at that, with a concern and affection for the younger generation which words cannot express, and with a faith in the sufficiency of Christ to bridge the distance Himself which equally defies language.

But in writing this book I have in mind the need of another group of people. It is that of many of my own generation who, having begun more or less where I began, and having lived through the years which I have witnessed, find themselves bereft of what is still my strength and stay—belief in life, faith in God, deep spiritual certainty. For the mystery to which I have to bear my testimony is not that I have been able to keep the Faith, but that the Faith has kept its hold on me. I am one of those whom life has not disillusioned even though it has again and again opened my eyes, hurt me, dismayed me, shamed and shocked me. I think it has done everything to me except allow me to turn on it and say in passionate sincerity, "I don't believe". What it has compelled me to do, sometimes against my will and against my reason, is to reaffirm with an equally passionate sincerity: "I can't help believing." It will clearly be beyond me to explain the "why" of this. As Pascal said: "The heart has its reasons which reason does not know." But I want to testify, as far as I can, to the "how" of it. And it is just possible that through the testimony some of the truth that goes beyond reason (above it, not below it) will manifest itself and do for others what—regardless of my deserts—it insists on doing for me.

At this point I will only add that, although I am deeply interested in theology, I am not a theologian and this book will in no sense be a theological essay. Certain great theological affirmations will, I believe, lie behind my testimony, but I content myself strictly with testimony— a personal endeavour to say in personal terms in what way life has kept me in the Faith.

CHAPTER TWO

HERITAGE

THIS book is testimony, not biography, but its argument cannot be presented apart from personal references of the kind in which I have already indulged. I will make these as slight as possible and keep them subordinate to their larger purpose.

In that distant universe of which I have spoken I came into an inheritance. It proved to be so productive that I cannot fairly assess my subsequent good fortune without taking it into account.

It all began in a mean street in Birmingham. There was a youth there who had received no formal education. By the time he was seven or eight he was working in a factory and the liberal education which he subsequently acquired —based on extraordinarily wide reading—was the result of a voracious desire to learn, aided by Cassell's penny-a-week *Self-Educator*. The lad's father had been an amiable drunkard and one of the child's responsibilities was to explore a circuit of public houses towards closing time and guide his father home. When the child reached young manhood he became a member of a gang of "Brummagem lads" who acquired some skill and reputation in the art of breaking up political meetings by storming the platform of the Bingley Hall, Birmingham. (Those were the days of John Bright's and Richard Cobden's oratory.) One Sunday night a few members of this gang found themselves outside Wesley Chapel, Constitution Hill, Birmingham, and they agreed to go inside and disturb the service. The result was that one of them—the youth whose story I have briefly told—was himself disturbed, in as sound a Methodist conversion as ever took place. The faith that came to him was tested through the next seventy years. It satisfied a mind that never ceased to be questioning and critical. It endured through unemployment and poverty, bereavement and disappointment, sickness and sorrows innumerable. Towards the end it flickered, through months and months of weariness and infirmity, but part of the flickering was due to impatience to be gone into that world of light in which for nearly three-quarters of a century he had firmly and eagerly believed.

In March, 1939, as I was setting out for the South Seas, I said goodbye to him, my father and my closest friend. We prayed together—he for blessings on my journey, I that he might soon be allowed to go upon his. Some months later I was on the island of Funafuti in the South Pacific when news of his death was cabled to me. I happened to be spending a few days alone in the bungalow of an absent government official. I had wanted to learn of my father's release, but when the word actually reached me I was for a time affected by a sense of utter solitariness more desperately chilling than I had ever believed possible. There was an old gramophone in the bungalow, a few well-worn records and some doubtful needles, but I found some Bach amongst the records and eventually I broke the silence. Before I next spoke to any human being I knew something about immortality and the fellowship of the Spirit which has so far proved absolutely unassailable.

This personal reference calls for one other before I pass from the personal to the more general. Shortly after my father's conversion he met in the same Wesley Chapel a shy young servant girl. The offer of a hymn-book brought them together and began a love-match which resulted in

my being blessed with a mother lovely—to my eyes and
heart—beyond compare. Poor, ill-treated in her childhood, almost illiterate (to the end of her life she could
only write with difficulty) she was possessed of an innate
culture as great as the heroism with which she shouldered
incredible burdens or as the beauty of spirit which gave
her sanctity in all our eyes. Life for her was hard to the
end; she died slaving to help someone whom she felt
could only be saved in that way. Yet for her, also, life
spelt fulfilment, joy, peace, and certainty. And neither
she nor her husband could explain why life had been so
rich for them save by attributing it to the grace of their
Lord Jesus Christ, the love of God and the fellowship
of the Holy Spirit.

Now I could have received this inheritance and been
grateful for it without thereby becoming possessed for
myself of that central certainty and intimacy of conviction which enables a man to say "I believe". What Thomas
Fuller* said of piety is true of that spiritual possession
which goes deeper than piety—religious conviction.
Meditating on the uncertain influence of heredity on character, Fuller wrote, in his *Scripture Observations:*

"Lord, I find the genealogy of my Saviour strangely
chequered with four remarkable changes in four immediate
generations:

"1. Rehoboam begat Abiam; that is, a bad father begat
a bad son.

"2. Abiam begat Asa; that is, a bad father a good son.

* Thomas Fuller (1608–1661), described by a contemporary biographer
—John Aubrey—as "a boy of pregnant wit", was a historian and divine
best known for his *Worthies of England*. When the times were dark he published *Good Thoughts in Bad Times*. When they became worse he wrote
Better Thoughts in Worse Times: and when most men thought the prospect
had improved, he offered them another sequel, *Mixt Contemplations in
Better Times*.

"3. Asa begat Jehoshaphat; that is, a good father a good son.

"4. Jehoshaphat begat Joram; that is, a good father a bad son.

"I see, Lord, from hence, that my father's piety cannot be entailed; that is bad news for me. But I see also that actual impiety is not always hereditary; that is good news for my son."

The truth is that in this great business of religious certitude we all reach a point where neither the example nor the authority of another can in itself kindle the vital spark and create faith. Respect for authority may lead us to accept certain religious truths as objective facts, just as a similar reliance on authority results in our accepting all manner of "truths"—scientific or historical, commonplace or exceptional—which we are not ourselves competent to prove. The same attitude to authority may induce us to adopt particular practices or ways of living as being religiously obligatory. The example of others, in belief or conduct, may also strengthen the claim which these truths make upon our acceptance. But the "belief" of which I am thinking lies at a point farther on than this. It goes beyond acceptance of truth and duty on the ground of authority or example. It is more inward in its compulsion and involves assents which go deeper than reason. It involves that power of thinking and believing with the whole self of which a great Spanish thinker wrote when he said:

"There are people who appear to think only with the brain, or with whatever may be the specific thinking organ; while others think with all the body and all the soul, with the blood, with the marrow of the bones, with the heart, with the lungs, with the belly, with the life."*

* Miguel de Unamuno : *The Tragic Sense of Life*, p. 14.

If belief of this depth and living quality is to be ours, it cannot be the result of a previous generation's experience The most vital element in it must touch us with a direct ness and a self-authenticating power which would be convincing, whether we happened to be the son of a Rehoboam or a Jehoshaphat.

Nevertheless, as I have acknowledged, I cannot treat my religious inheritance as unrelated to my own subsequent experience—any more than I can cease to be grateful for so inestimable a blessing. If the gift of faith, in the direct sense of which I have been speaking, had never become mine, I still think I should have had to take into account what had happened to my father—and not only to my father but to countless others of his and of preceding generations. I should, in fact, have had to reckon with the great Christian tradition in its central testimony to the presence in life of a living God, acting upon men with saving and re-assuring power. I was richly fortunate in that this most vivid and living quality in the Christian tradition had reached my own home. It was, indeed, a marvellous thing that the fountain of the water of life should have played in the backyard of a little shop in Birmingham in the twentieth century, so that grace could seem to me as fresh and near as that. But even this would have been less convincing—I might have regarded it as an illusion—if I could not have related it to recorded evidence more widespread and with a larger history than the personal testimony of my parents only.

I know we differ greatly from one another in our "sense of the past", our feeling for history, our instinctive reverence for the mightiest things that happened in the centuries preceding the moment when this planet was blessed with our presence on it. But I think a good many people would be the better and the steadier if in their reflective moments they set their thought about these present harsh and hectic years within the longer perspectives of history. I often take to my comfort and rebuke the advice which an Oxford teacher gave me after I had submitted to his judgment a notion which, I thought, was based on a fairly long view of things. After the manner of his kind he carefully avoided telling me I was hasty and superficial. Instead he gave to my views a polite and acidly qualified approval. "Yes," he said, "a valid judgment, perhaps, if you are thinking in decades; but in matters of this kind think in centuries, think in centuries!"

Why not? It is, in fact, against a background as historically spacious as this that the drama of our individual lives and our particular age is set. And—to say the least about it—one of the brightest and noblest features of the background is what we call the Christian tradition. From the heart of it there proceed the mighty assurances that God reigns, that history is within His keeping, and that the future belongs to Him. At its luminous centre there is the faith that the coming of Jesus Christ into history did something more than add one more to the long procession of seekers after truth; it signified an authentic disclosure of truth itself. It was the act of God "from the other side", a breaking into these dimensions of time and space from that transcendent realm where the key to the mystery lies. The historical events to which this assurance is related include circumstances most damnable, men at their worst, premature death and the suffering of the innocent; but these events are dealt with by a power which takes the sting out of death, offers balm for sorrow and forgiveness for sin, teaches us how to live in this world and kindles a lively faith in the world to come.

Of course I have always had to reckon with the possibility that all this might be an illusion and that the Christian tradition, with the rest of history, is "bunk". I think I came nearest to accepting this soul-destroying conclusion at a time when Bertrand Russell's earlier brilliance was fascinating my generation. That I nearly did so was due, I think, more than anything to the fact that Russell found language in which to express his unbelief as hauntingly beautiful as the language of faith! I confess that a recent re-reading of some of the familiar passages after an interval of twenty-five years has left me more critical of a scientist's rhetoric than envious of his power of expression, especially in the once-famous essay on "A Free Man's Worship". But such lines as the following recall the potent influence of which I have been speaking:

"Brief and powerless is Man's life; on him and on all his race the slow, sure doom falls pitiless and dark. Blind to good and evil, reckless of destruction, omnipotent matter rolls on its relentless way; for Man, condemned today to lose his dearest, tomorrow himself to pass through the gate of darkness, it remains only to cherish, ere yet the blow falls, the lofty thoughts that ennoble his little day; disdaining the coward terrors of the slave of Fate, to worship at the shrine that his own hands have built; undismayed by the empire of chance, to preserve a mind free from the wanton tyranny that rules his outward life; proudly defiant of the irresistible forces that tolerate, for a moment, his knowledge and his condemnation, to sustain alone, a weary but unyielding Atlas, the world that his own ideals have fashioned despite the trampling march of unconscious power.

"That Man is the product of causes which had no prevision of the end they were achieving; that his origin, his growth, his hopes and fears, his loves and beliefs, are but the outcome of accidental collocations of atoms; that no fire, no heroism, no intensity of thought and feeling, can preserve an individual life beyond the grave; that all the labours of the ages, all the devotion, all the inspiration, all the noonday brightness of human genius, are destined to extinction in the vast death of the solar system, and that the whole temple of Man's achievement must inevitably be buried beneath the débris of a universe in ruins—all these things, if not quite beyond dispute, are yet so nearly certain, that no philosophy which rejects them can hope to stand. Only within the scaffolding of these truths, only on the firm foundation of unyielding despair, can the soul's habitation henceforth be safely built."*

When I first read this essay I could have nothing but a novice's respect for the scientific and philosophical knowledge of the writer and by nature I was then disposed to accord him even greater homage for his fashioning of rhythmic prose. Yet when I found a scientist and philosopher allowing himself to accord to "unyielding despair" the dignity of a "firm foundation", for me the spell was broken. In my lighter moods I have set against this passage the advice of the philosophically-minded bookmaker: "Don't make Despair first favourite. 'Edge a bit on 'Ope." Most seriously I have weighed the authority of the Bertrand Russells against that of the Hebrew Prophets, the writers of the four Gospels and *Acts*, St. Paul, St. Augustine, St. Thomas Aquinas, Milton, Bach and Handel, and the countless scholars and artificers in words who have believed in the Word made flesh; and I have never been able to feel that it is ignoble or self-deluding to place some reliance on these when either I doubt the validity of my own religious experience or happen to be passing through a dry season spiritually. I have, in fact, unashamedly rested on the Christian tradition. As I have already emphasized, the tradition cannot create a living faith, but it is a constant illuminant to the personal experience and makes this more than the private

*Bertrand Russell: *Mysticism and Logic and Other Essays.*

and peculiar possession of an individual. Further, it brings correctives and disciplines to bear on the personal experience and by the discipline makes for spiritual enrichment. Most important of all, it keeps leading the individual out of pre-occupation with what he or she has "felt" (or hasn't "felt") into greater attentiveness towards the whole range of God's dealings with mankind and to the ever-growing wonder of His own nature and purpose.

CHAPTER THREE

GOD, HISTORY AND ME

(1)

I HAVE gratefully acknowledged my debt to parents who themselves constituted for me such a convincing introduction to a knowledge of Christianity. But that larger Christian tradition, which I soon knew to be authenticated by more weighty evidence than the testimony of a single home, was made known to me through agencies accessible to others as well as to myself. In this chapter and the next I speak about two of those agencies and their relation to my own religious certainty —namely, the testimony of the Bible and the ministrations of the Church. Both these themes—especially in their more than personal reference—could be treated at far greater length than is possible in this book. In particular, an adequate discussion of the authority of the Bible in the sphere of Christian conviction and experience, its essential message and the ways in which it can best be used in the nurture of the spiritual life—all these are matters which would require volumes rather than a single chapter and here I make no attempt even to touch upon them. I confine my testimony to certain selected points at which I find the influence and authority of the Bible crucial to my growth in Christian certainty.

The evangelical experience which lay at the heart of my home life was combined—rather unusually for those days —with an attitude to the Bible which encouraged a book-loving family to treat it "as you would treat any other book". It was a common family grievance that this advice was made difficult to follow by the usual appearance of the Book—dismal bindings, small type, and the tiresome cutting of natural paragraphs—even sentences—into "verses". (The strain of these things upon my radical father's devotional temper was aggravated every time he caught sight of the dedication of the Authorized Version to "the Most High and Mighty Prince James", with his "many singular and extraordinary graces".) This free and critical approach was not confined to externals. We knew many passages in the Old Testament which could never sustain any natural association in our thinking with either holiness or inspiration. The morals of the patriarchs did not impress us and when we first read Quiller Couch's *Art of Reading* and there found it roundly asserted that whatever else the story of Jacob and Esau demonstrated it was clear that "Esau was a gentleman: Jacob was not", "Q" became one of our most respected expositors.

This attitude must be clearly distinguished from flippancy, irreverence or any secularist atmosphere. I must keep emphasizing the evangelical warmth and piety within which this liberty was enjoyed. This carried with it disciplines and checks upon our freedom which were most obediently heeded. To ill-treat any book by careless handling was a social offence. To mishandle a copy of the Bible was a major misdemeanour. In a family which enjoyed wit, biblical parodies were taboo and we were cautioned never to tolerate "detestable imitations of Holy Writ".

I dwell on all this in order to emphasize something which has played its part amongst the many means of grace to which I have been indebted. This was a sense of freedom in reading Scripture which made me feel at home with the Bible. Although I have come to venerate it because it is like no other book in the world, I trace the beginning of its authority over me to the fact that, handled with freedom by a young book-lover, it could hold its own with all other books in the world. I have known—as so many others have experienced—barren periods in my use of it. There have been times when it has fallen into neglect as a devotional companion even while I have continued to work with it as a text-book. But again and again it has proved to be the rock on which my faith has rested and the spring at which it has been renewed. There are few hymns in which I join with greater sincerity than those which testify to its power.

> It is the chart and compass
> That o'er life's surging sea,
> Mid mists and rocks and quicksands,
> Still guides, O Christ, to Thee.

Out of this early freedom in the handling of the Bible, coupled with reverence towards its central testimony, certain assumptions and attitudes of mind began to determine my religious thinking. In this attempt to make them explicit I am probably reading back into earlier stages conclusions which only became definite later on, but the manner of their growth matters little; my purpose is to indicate what, for me, a "biblical faith" has come to mean.

First, my thought of God has always been in very personal terms. He has never become an abstraction only, a "first principle" or impersonal "absolute". Faith has involved a very personal relationship to a very personal God. This is one of the chief characteristics of all biblical discussion of God. Amidst the diversities of experience and viewpoint represented in the literature which constitutes the Bible the dominant assumption is that God is personal and is to be known in personal terms. Throughout the growth in knowledge of God which the Bible illustrates—from a tribal deity to the God and Father of our Lord Jesus Christ—it is taken for granted that the full truth about God is truth about a Person, not a Principle only. Of course, much biblical writing about God is "anthropomorphic" in the sense that human categories are being employed to describe what clearly goes beyond all human categories. Their use, therefore, has obvious limitations. The result may be no more than a childish sketch of what will continue to baffle the maturest art. And the earlier sketches—made before the artists could work by the light given in Jesus Christ—contain error and distortion. But while the revelation of God in Christ corrects the errors, it confirms the central assumption that true thinking about God is personal thinking.

As the years have passed, my sense of the ultimate mystery of the Godhead has deepened. The mystery has a luminous centre—Jesus. I see the glory of God in the face of Jesus Christ and I know that from the heart of the mystery Person speaks to persons. I can hold to this assurance—or be held by it—while acknowledging that within the total mystery there are truths about the nature of Godhead that may go "beyond personality", if there be anything good and holy and true that is, in fact, "beyond" it. I can understand why the Church which is founded on acknowledgment of the Divinity of Christ has nevertheless found itself compelled to assert that Jesus alone is not the Godhead; only when we see Him as one with God the Father and God the Holy Spirit do we see the mystery in its true proportions. I can, further, accept the doctrine of the Trinity as yet another instance of the use of categories which illustrate or adumbrate the truth without being adequate wholly to define it. Here again, in the attempt to elucidate mysteries which go beyond these dimensions of time and space, human expression remains relatively childish. But so long as it holds to the conviction that at the core of the mystery there is *personal* divinity (which—amongst much else—is what the doctrine of the Trinity does), its spiritual discernment is in line with the ultimate truth of the matter. This—as I have said—is a characteristically biblical attitude, having the highest sanction we know—that of Jesus Christ. So for me the Bible has kept all my religious thinking within personal terms.

I must, however, emphasize the fact that in using a phrase like "religious thinking" I am referring to something more than a rational or theorizing process. Such reasoning powers as I possess are not inactive in my religious experience. I nurture faith as well as stretch my mind by following as far as I can the debates of the theologians. But I have long known that intellectual awareness is different from conviction. Truth, seen by reason, only passes into conviction when it has been appropriated, acted upon and trusted with a wholeness of personal response which includes much more than reason. This "more" extends to the will; it involves the imagination and the affections. It means bringing into play the total "yielding" capacity of our natures—the submissive element which not only issues in practical obedience but gives a deep personal assent involving heart as well as mind. I have already touched on this in the preceding chapter and it is an emphasis which will be bound to recur in this book. What I here stress is its relation to my thinking of God in personal terms. I have known that what this involves is not only my reason's acceptance of a hypothesis that God is personal. It requires an essentially personal attitude on my part—I would rather call it a personal deference—to the fact of a Personal God.

For me, life's supreme interest and importance keep

turning on the fact that to be really alive means to be living amongst people. I can have too much of them—as we
all can, and I generally find myself wanting a larger
amount of solitude than most other people seem to need.
But real living is being with folk, aware of them, sensitive
to them, interested in them. The most lifeless moments I
have known have been in some far distant places of the
earth where even nature's loveliness and grandeur have
chilled me because there has been no sign of human
habitation. If I have there found companionship in a book
it has been because there are always persons behind words,
but even solitariness tempered by the written word is not
enough to make life *life*; sooner or later I have needed
the living person with whom to share the living word.
Then, the need met, the setting has taken on a new meaning; because of its personal foreground, the whole scene
—including nature's loveliness—has "come alive" with a
power of contentment that the soul needs. Now all this,
I believe, is bound up with the fact that at the heart of this
mysterious universe—at the heart of the mystery of God
—there is personal Deity. And I have put this to the test
with that response which is more than the assent of reason.
Taking for granted this fact of a personal God I have let
my deepest personal need go out to it, and the result has
been communion. That is why I know that I need never
feel finally alone in solitariness. Though flesh and blood
may cry out for the sight of a person amidst some scene of
nature's unpeopled grandeur, I have known a personal
answer satisfying to faith if not to sight. And if—as can
frequently happen in this world of curiously assorted
people—my solitariness has been fretted rather than eased
by the sight of certain human beings, well—a better
personal response to my need (with some corrective to its
"imperfect sympathies") has not been lacking as I have

walked with God. Anthropomorphic, no doubt, but spiritually not erroneous with its sanction in a biblical faith.

(II)

This habit of attuning my religious thinking to the assumptions and affirmations of the Bible has had another consequence for faith. It has meant that, despite the course of events through the last few decades, I have not been able to surrender the conviction that history has a meaning and that the last word on all that happens in this world lies with God. I have lived through years—as we all have—in which it has seemed that most of the larger happenings in the world have run counter to any purpose of goodness. They have been a denial of all that we can mean when we speak of the "love of God". Further, I know that we have now quite soberly to reckon with the possibility that worse may yet come. History having brought us to the "Era of Atomic Power", it is not out of the question that this era will see the end of "Christian civilization", with all the charities and decencies, the mercies and integrities which have hitherto gathered around that rather indefinable but very meaningful phrase. I am well aware that to go on in face of all this and yet to attach "meaning" to history—especially a meaning that can be related to the over-ruling providence of the God and Father of our Lord Jesus Christ—is to make a heavy demand on reason. I can only affirm again that both demand and response involve more than reason; they engage the whole person and do so in the power of truth which will ultimately accord with reason when reason is in a position to see all the facts and base its judgment on wisdom as well as rationality.

I am here dealing with issues which I frankly admit I

cannot compass. All I can do is to testify to certain guiding factors in my continuing thought on these matters, especially those which I chiefly owe to the influence of the Bible.

It is a commonplace to say that the Bible deals with the "stuff of history". Of course it draws into its orbit and for its own central purpose legend as well as history, mythology and poetry, story and song. But the central core of the revealing process to which the Bible testifies is a core of history. God has "meant business" in the creation of this world. The rise and fall of nations is not a haphazard affair. The peculiar position of Israel in history is not fortuitous. The supreme event in all history—the coming of Jesus Christ—is a happening in the fulness of the times; it occurred with a timeliness that was of God's deciding. Henceforth there is to be seen in this event the clue to the interpretation of history, and in its light the happenings of our time can be seen in their true perspective and abiding significance.

Yet although events accompanying the march of time in this world can thus be read with meaning, the setting of the whole process is in eternity, not time. This world-scene, though very real, is not the final reality. Always it must be looked upon from a standpoint which never ceases to take into account the existence of a realm, an order, a Kingdom which will endure when the fashion of this world has passed away.

Such, in brief, is for me the biblical attitude to history. It is pre-eminently a New Testament attitude, for the central ground of the faith on which it is based is the fact of Jesus Christ. Yet—and this remains one of the marvels of history—there was manifest in the pre-Christian history of Israel, supremely through that unique succession of spiritual geniuses the Hebrew prophets,

an outlook and a faith in the future which make for
continuity between the pre-Christian and Christian verdicts on history which are enshrined in the Bible. This is
far from attributing to any of the Old Testament writers
an inerrancy of judgment or a fully-informed Christian
insight into the events which they were witnessing. It
does acknowledge, however, in the Bible as a whole,
a standpoint, a spirit, a sense of what is finally significant
and a faith in the ultimate rightness of things, which are
characteristic of a Christian view of history.

In the application of this faith to the happenings of their
time the biblical writers clearly record judgments which
are often more relative than absolute in their value. The
Old Testament historians, for example, were working
with limited data at their disposal and on a comparatively
small canvas. It is true that the standpoint from which
they wrote led them to set the events which they were
handling within a movement beginning with the dawn of
history and the spring-time of creation. But although
there are hints that they knew more than we sometimes
suppose about what had happened and was happening
outside the Mediterranean world, much more had yet to
be known and understood about the total course of
human history hitherto. Like historians of many other
ages, including those who have worked with more
"scientific" instruments at their disposal, they were disposed to see in the fortunes and achievements of their
own countrymen the only thread that matters in the
whole pattern of history. Yet alongside all this, three other
facts at least have to be reckoned with. First, even upon
that larger canvas which later and fuller knowledge makes
it possible to use, the history of the Hebrews does not
slip into insignificance. It remains at least one of the
crucial threads—indeed, the crucial thread—within the

larger pattern. Secondly, not even an excessive national pride and sense of particularity hindered the recorders of Hebrew history from bringing their own people under the condemnation of historical judgments. Again, one of the astonishments of history is provided by this power of radical self-criticism which the biblical historians derived from loyalties more than national, from moral values and spiritual insights which have remained significant for subsequent generations and other civilizations. The climax of this self-critical and supra-national approach to history was reached in the New Testament with that Hebrew of the Hebrews, Paul. For him the Jewish rejection of Jesus came to mean that the central stream of God's revealing and saving purpose for mankind, hitherto running through the story of Israel, would henceforth pass into a "new Israel", drawn chiefly from the non-Jewish or Gentile world and cutting across all racial and national distinctions. Thirdly, the story of the race which cradled Jesus Christ and with whose history His revelation was so closely interwoven, cannot be other than of supreme significance for all ages and peoples. To say no more about it than this, historians of other races and cultures find it increasingly necessary to take notice of the place of Jesus Christ in world history. And the abiding value of the work of the historians of the Old Testament lies in the fact that, with all their limitations of knowledge and judgment, they persistently read the signs of the times in the light of a purpose which found its inevitable culmination (even where it proved to be a radical corrective) in the Christian revelation.

It is not my purpose in this book to attempt even a summary presentation of the way in which the writers of the Bible apply to the events of their time what we may now call the biblical approach to history. I want now to return to the personal testimony which I am making and to show how, with this biblical faith in history as the background of my thinking, I have been able to see reason even in the events through which my own generation has passed and is passing.

My starting point lies in acceptance of the fact that only within the setting of eternity can we ever expect to make sense of the course of events within this world. This is not just a private escape from a problem which has defeated me. It is a personal appropriation of a conviction which has been either the presupposition or the conclusion of the most serious thinkers of all ages. It is an acceptance of something which is axiomatic for all the greatest religions and which has given the deepest and most moving tones to all artistic achievement. The native habitat of this creature man, who can think and dream and aspire and conceive of goodness and justice and immortality, is in dimensions other than these. The final fulfilment of human destiny is in worlds beyond this. In eternity and the life-to-come there lies the goal to which history is moving. Scarcely a page of the New Testament can be read without this assertion being driven home. In acceptance of it I find the sense of proportion within which to set the obstinate questionings and continued wrestling with the dilemmas raised by experience here.

This has never meant for me simply a postponement of thought on contemporary problems or any kind of assumption that it doesn't matter what happens in this world (especially to other people); it will all come out right in the end. Again, I have learned from the Bible habitually to regard the present as being of life-and-death importance, just because there is eternity to reckon with and a destiny which will embrace other worlds than this.

Wrong choices and wrong acts, whether by individuals
or communities, are desperately serious and their consequences can never be easily annulled. The sorry tale of
wrong which runs like a dark stain through all history
and has made so terribly sombre the chronicle of our own
time will have to be reckoned with in this moral universe.
I do not know, and cannot here know, through what process of expiation the wrong-doers of the past (in community and in their individual wrong) are passing in other
worlds than this. I only know that neither they nor I
can escape it and that in so far as it proves to be endurable
it will be because God's mercy alone will make it more
redemptive than punitive. I cannot conceive (again, with
thought anchored to the Bible) that either here or here-
after is it possible for us to know in experience that God
is more concerned to redeem than punish the wrong-doer
save in an utterly lowly and penitential acceptance of the
judgment and mercy with which we are confronted in
Christ. And I know, by foretaste as well as by conviction,
that acceptance of love's mercy and redeeming power
(whether direct from God or in any human relationship
which has been set right by grace) proves that life holds
no more searching and costly experience than that of
being forgiven.

> *Learn that the flame of the Everlasting Love*
> *Doth burn ere it transform.*

I believe then, that the drama of history is set within an
eternal destiny in which men, as individuals and members
of community, are free to make wrong choices though
never finally to escape the consequences of their choice.
The fact that the Christian revelation enables us to look to
redemption rather than condemnation as the last word
on the matter does not make life any less responsible.

That pre-Christian word of the Psalmist expresses a spiritual insight which the Christian revelation makes more profoundly true.

> *There is forgiveness with Thee,*
> *That Thou mayest be feared.*

This element of freedom in human history, though ultimately subject to a moral universe, means first, that the detailed happenings of any particular period are not the result of some pre-determined scheme. That God has a purpose in history does not require as its corollary a view of man which makes us nothing but automata. Morally and spiritually, the divine purpose is all the greater because it requires for its fulfilment the free response of creatures who may refuse to co-operate and may thereby thwart, for the time being, the good purpose of God. Secondly, this very fact means that again and again it may be the lot of a particular generation or a particular group of people to live through a "thwarting" period. This plunges us at once into the awful problem of the suffering of the innocent and the enmeshing of the individual in events over which the individual alone is powerless to exercise a decisive influence. There is no glib solution of this problem and I am not pretending that I have found one. I can see, not least from the teaching of the Hebrew prophets and still more from the content of the New Testament (especially from such profound comments on the nature of life as the Epistles to the Corinthians and Ephesians offer), that being a "person" involves relationships with other persons at a depth where interdependence is of the stuff of life. Being "bound in the bundle of life" (to use an Old Testament phrase) or being "members one of another" (in New Testament parlance) is the source of life's highest ecstasies as well as its sharpest agonies.

Again, when I reflect on the way in which, in the deepest relationships between persons, there are moments when even the suffering of the innocent can be creative and redemptive, I am prevented from letting this heart-burdening problem constitute merely a proof that the universe is either malignant or meaningless. Still more as I dwell on the extent to which the unique place of Jesus in history and in the religious experience of mankind is bound up with His personal acceptance of unmerited suffering and His faith that through this way alone could certain spiritual forces become operative, I find it the more easy—I would say, the more imperative—to go on in faith that there is a meaning to this element in life which will find its vindication in a process which has eternity as its context.

It is on the basis of such thinking as this, the primary authority for which is a biblical authority, that I have found it possible, without disillusionment or bitterness, to live through two world wars, their uneasy intervening peace, and this later tragic aftermath of weariness, sorrow and fear. To put it simply and even crudely: I cannot blame God for the mess we are in. I cannot wish that by some almighty intervening act, not requiring for its efficacy the free response of men and women who have it in them to choose, He would change the course of events for us. Although I have shared, with a good many other relatively innocent people (I can only say, *relatively* innocent) dangers, sufferings and fears which our corporate sins have brought upon us, I am less disposed to quarrel with the universe than I am to recognize how responsible a business it is to be alive and how pathetic it is that with the lessons of history before us, the example and Gospel of Christ as our guide and strength, we are taking so long to learn to live in this world as citizens of eternity and in the grace and dignity of children of God.

For though we are free, with a freedom which carries consequences against which I believe we have no right to whimper, history is something more than the record of undirected free actions, wayward because no guide to better living has been offered. Again, a biblical faith begins with a God who reveals Himself and offers guidance, whether or not the guidance is followed. He has not left Himself without witness. There is a light that lighteth every man coming into the world. Seers and prophets, moralists and teachers have appeared in every age, and to every generation has been given some insight into a way of life which, if followed, would have kept humanity from some of its perils and lifted it nearer the fulfilment of the purpose for which it has been created. Most significant of all, God's self-revealing activity has reached its climax in One who for all mankind is the Way, the Truth and the Life. We know in Him to what end our freedom should be directed, what is our life's supreme, saving choice.

I write this from the Christian standpoint, and the biblical presuppositions of my thinking give a central place to that revealing process which used the history of the Hebrews and the spiritual genius of their prophets (under whose influence what we call the historical books of the Bible were written) as a unique preparation for the supreme disclosure of God's purpose in Jesus Christ. It is not my intention to discuss the relation of the non-Christian religions to the Christian revelation, or the significance of the religious quest and spiritual achievements of other races and peoples, but a slight reference to this great subject is relevant to my argument at this point.

First—though I make this observation little more than in passing—while I am convinced of the central place which the history of that "peculiar" people, the Hebrews, has occupied in the revelation of God and the disclosure of His purpose, it seems to me no less certain that there must be a "peculiar" rôle, a distinctive part, for all peoples to play both in the full understanding of God's purpose and its ultimate fulfilment. I believe that this rôle does not become clearly manifest nor fully operative until the light of Christ has been brought to bear upon a nation's or a race's heritage, gifts and characteristics. I further believe that the meaning of it is missed (as it was missed by the Jews) the moment that a "peculiar" calling is interpreted in terms of privilege rather than service to the whole body of mankind. One of the mighty obligations and potentialities of Christian missionary activity is this illuminating of other people's destinies through the lifting up of Christ and the quickening of a response which, amongst other things, will hasten the accomplishment of God's good purpose for the whole family of mankind. Tardiness in fulfilling this missionary obligation to go into all the world with the saving news is, in the long run, the most grievous failure of all, for it occurs at the point where the greatest light of Revelation has shone.

My second observation relates to the fact that in most of the great non-Christian religions there are included moral codes which, if accepted with full obedience, would have taken humanity far higher in moral achievement than it has yet reached. In certain particulars the precepts of the world's great moralists often resemble one another and where they have been followed and made a living part of the structure of great civilizations they have resulted in those chapters in human history which have been marked by a large degree of happiness, achievement and peace. This is not to say that "all religions are the same". Similarities in moral codes are not the same as similarities in religious insights and convictions. Religion, though it includes morals, is wider and deeper in its range. Primarily it deals with the nature of God and the character of the spiritual universe. It touches the springs of morality, points to the ultimate and eternal reasons *why* certain moral standards are imperative, and concerns itself with the question *how* moral ideals can be realized. In all these respects, as well as in some essential features of its moral teaching, there is an enormous and most radical difference between Christianity and the non-Christian religions. In drawing attention to certain similarities rather than contrasts between the moral codes embodied in other religions, my point here is simply to emphasize the fact that in the exercise of its freedom mankind as a whole has not been without guidance, to which a religious and otherworldly sanction has been attached, and which has largely contributed to such happiness as has been enjoyed. With fuller obedience there would have been greater happiness. The tragic element in history has been the difference in every age between the precepts of its greatest teachers and the practice of the age.

> *Knowledge we ask not—knowledge Thou hast lent,*
> *But, Lord, the will—there lies our bitter need,*
> *Give us to build above the deep intent*
> *The deed, the deed.* [1]

To this situation Christianity has a word to say and a power to offer which sets it in an entirely different category from all other religions, but again I would stress the fact that this unique revelation, Christianity, comes to us from a God whose essential nature it is to reveal Himself and to whose purpose all history contains testimony.

What is that purpose? To what sort of result within

[1] "A Prayer," by John Drinkwater. By permission of Sidgwick & Jackson Ltd.

this scene of history has the purpose of God been moving? To what end should the free choices of men, made in response to revelation, have led?

I believe the answer to these questions must take into account two great terms. One is "the Christian Church". The other is "Christian civilization". I shall speak about the Church in the next chapter. In the remainder of this chapter I shall speak of "Christian civilization" as representing something of what we are meant to achieve so long as we inhabit this world.

In using the phrase "Christian civilization" I must reiterate the fact that the full sweep of God's purpose for man goes beyond this world. No "civilization" here can therefore contain it. The biblical term is not "civilization" but "Kingdom", the Kingdom in which God's sovereignty is fully acknowledged and His will obeyed. Although both Old and New Testaments clearly envisage a more perfect realization of this Kingdom within history, its full scope is just as clearly anticipated only in an age beyond this. But so long as these are our perspectives, it is possible to use the phrase "Christian civilization" to describe one great aspect of the life of the Kingdom which it is God's good pleasure that we should enjoy here.

Now, it is sadly evident that no generation has yet achieved or experienced in all its possible richness this interim life of the Kingdom which I am describing by the phrase "Christian civilization". Even in the nobler periods of history life for too many people has lacked much that would belong to it were man's acceptance of and obedience to the Reign of God complete. Moreover, by its very nature a truly Christian civilization would always be more dynamic than static; its order and characteristics could not be stabilized or frozen at a particular period so that we could say, "This is it and this may be accepted as the pattern for all time." A truly Christian way of life, one that reflects something of the splendour of eternity and has the Holy Spirit for its dynamic, will always be more creative than fixed. Yet here and there throughout the course of history there have been moments when great approximations to this ideal have been attained and when some of the implications of the claims of the Kingdom have been embodied in the laws and customs, the culture and behaviour of earthly kingdoms.

A discussion of the extent to which genuine approximations to fulness of life in this world have appeared within civilizations not directly influenced by the historic Christian revelation is, again, a matter beyond the scope of this book. Clearly there are elements in great civilizations of the past and in some contemporary civilizations of the East which suggest that the light which lighteth every man has "at sundry times and in divers manners" resulted in insights and obediences, especially in the realms of creative beauty and of social behaviour, which should enter into any full appropriation of the life of the Kingdom in this world. In any case, it is significant that what has been commonly called Christian civilization in the West has been compounded of much that had its origin apart from historic Christianity. The Hebrew tradition (which had itself made cultural appropriations from other ancient civilizations) contributed, amongst much else, its strong sense of social justice and its conception of personal integrity. First-century Christianity drew to itself innumerable elements from both the Graeco-Oriental and the Graeco-Roman worlds, and the same process continued through the building up of the great mediaeval society of the West. In the modern period this creative incorporation of fresh elements within Christian civilization has laid under tribute features characteristic both of modern Europe and America and it has begun to draw enrichment from the Orient. But in our own time a point has been reached where, instead of being able to assume that in a world in which knowledge of Christ has become as widespread as it is today the natural development of civilization means the natural development of *Christian* civilization, we are compelled to ask whether mankind as a whole is not farther from the Kingdom than it has been for many generations.

The most obvious reasons for asking this question are provided by two world wars and a peace in which we can find it possible to talk about a third. But behind these lurid symptoms there are reasons which require further analysis.

First, it has long been clear to the more reflective minds that "civilizing", in the commonly accepted interpretation of the word, may have no relation whatever to experience of life in the Kingdom of God or to the fashioning of a Christian civilization. Men may be provided with the means of mastering their environment; they may be able to handle more and more of the resources of this world; there may come to them increase of leisure, health and wealth; they may become more independent and better educated (again in a commonly accepted use of the term which may, nevertheless, be open to fundamental criticism); but with all this, unless the main note to which life is set is one that puts knowledge of God and His will as man's supreme concern, obedience to Him as our preeminent responsibility, "civilization" may, in fact, mean regression rather than progress. Our age has not lacked prophetic voices declaring this truth, nor has this word of prophecy been uttered only from the Church's pulpits. What we have lacked more than prophecy has been obedience.

A second factor, bound up with the first, arises from

the speed and success with which, through recent generations, man's mastery of "things" has dominated the rest of
life. This is an age of unprecedented technical competence
and power, a consequence, in the main, of the scientific
era which is the setting of modern history. To speak of
this in derogatory terms and to suggest that by its very
nature it runs counter to Christian obedience or a Christian
view of the universe is, of course, quite wrong. Discovery
is only one aspect of revelation and the age of science is
one of the great ages of revelation. Further, it is accompanied by another feature of revelation—the entrusting
of men with new power intended to make for fulness of
living. If the doctrine of the Holy Spirit had been more
adequately handled by theologians during the last fifty
years (in company with scientists who were also Christians)
there might have been averted not only the great separa-
tion in thought between science and religion, but that
purely secular use of the astonishing mechanics of our
age which is the root of so much of our disorder. Where
we have gone wrong has been in our divorce of the idea of
"discovery" from that of "revelation". We have gloried
in the human aptitude for discovery without realizing
that, after all, it is only one of the processes by which we
receive revelation. It is still necessary—in fact it becomes
increasingly so—to pay heed to the essential character
of the universe which is thus disclosing itself, and this
requires more than the scientific techniques of the dis-
coverer. It needs the attitude of mind of the poet and
artist and most of all the reverent, obedient and humble
qualities of the religious spirit. Our growing sense of
mastery over things needs to be accompanied by a more
sensitive concern than ever to know to what ends God
intends this mastery to be exercised. Lacking this concern, with all the self-disciplines that go with it, the most

characteristic feature of our age has been a sense of power divorced from reverence towards God. From this there has followed what is virtually a self-deification of man, and it is this—idolatry in its most destructive form—that has lain behind some of the most terrible and tragic happenings of our time.

This leads me to a recognition of the most dangerous and least rational of all elements in life as we know it today—the manifestation by man himself of powers and qualities more savage than civilized in their nature and undisciplined by acceptance of any final authority outside his own likes or dislikes, his ambitions or fears. The phenomenon itself is not new, of course. It is as old as human nature. But its present manifestation, not only in individuals but in societies, and the coupling of it with that mastery over things which gives it coercive and destructive possibilities on a scale hitherto unequalled, constitute the heart of our peril and the gravity of this particular period in history. Here I return to the point which I have already touched upon in passing—namely, the serious likelihood that by our misuse of freedom and disregard of any moral authority rooted in the eternities, "history" may soon witness the end of any attempt to embody within the structure of this world the life of the Kingdom of God. We may choose the way of destruction with a finality which may be irredeemable so far as life on this planet is concerned.

The recognition of as grave a possibility as this is, I believe, demanded by a Christian view of life and a Christian interpretation of history. Again, it is an attitude which is one with the biblical view of history. Our time here is but a sojourning. When its purpose is truly fulfilled it gives us a foretaste of the life of the Kingdom; we achieve in right human relationships, through right relationship with God, a life in fellowship which reflects something of that eternal realm within which the whole process is set. But always—so the Bible constantly recognizes—the disobedience of individuals and nations may result in a world that is the negation of the Kingdom, and for whole communities if not for the whole body of mankind, the scene may be shifted from this world in some final cataclysm.

It is true that the Bible contemplates the end of history as the result of something other than human disobedience. Indeed, it eagerly anticipates that end as the outcome of our obedience and the climax of God's good purpose for us. Life here is only a prelude to the splendours which we may well long for with impatience. Hope, not despair, thus belongs to the biblical doctrine of the "end". Yet, running through this teaching of an end which will be the climax of a good purpose, there is the very different note of a disastrous close which may be precipitated by sin, with judgment and expiation to follow. It is as though man can press the misuse of his freedom to lengths which must result in a radical re-setting of the arena within which the drama of our redemption is worked out.

We ought not, even in the darkest times, to turn the biblical teaching regarding the end of history into a prophecy of doom. A more authentic proclamation of the saving goodness of God and of the glorious purpose which "history" was intended to hasten, may well be the message which we need above all others to hear and make known at the present time. The goodness of God might then lead us to repentance. Yet the stern and astringent note which accompanies even the biblical doctrine of hope cannot be absent from Christian prophecy today.

Personally I take so sombre a view of the events

through which I have lived and of the mood of men in general just now that I am bound to regard it as a certainty that, "except we repent" the closure will be moved in judgment upon the history of civilization in this world. Where "pessimism" of this sort differs from that of the sceptic lies, first, in the phrase which I have just used— "except we repent", and secondly in the certainty, to which I have already given frequent expression, that the whole process, in time and in eternity, lies in the hands of God and that neither death nor life can take us beyond His purpose and its ultimate fulfilment. This carries with it a responsible view of life after death and of the process by which we may be redeemed in realms beyond this into the way of obedience; but even the sternest tones which belong to this truth are but part of that total theme which speaks of the Majesty of God and of a redeeming love to which will belong the last word upon the story of mankind.

Although I find it possible to contemplate the worst as happening within the sphere of history and to contemplate it not only without loss of faith but *because* of faith and faith's biblical foundations, I must again assert that this carries active, and not merely passive, consequences for conduct. I have dwelt on those tragic elements in the present situation which are presented by our misuse of freedom, our wrong choices and the use of power undisciplined by reverence and spiritual obedience. These are the root causes of the *malaise* from which the whole world is suffering and repentance in relation to them is our primary spiritual need. But bound up with these things and partly expressive of them, there are particular failures in the disordered life of our time, the heeding of which, in terms of political and social action, is a necessary part of our repentance.

I have already acknowledged that, despite the use I have made of the term "Christian civilization", the full realization of what this goal should mean has never yet been achieved—not even in the "ages of faith" or in the more peaceful or apparently more contented eras of history. In today's disorder I believe we are being shown, amongst much else, certain of the reasons why civilization hitherto—even where we have claimed for it the term "Christian"—has fallen lamentably short of that interim life of the Kingdom which a Christian civilization would embody. Here I point briefly to two of these "lessons of history".

The first has its symptom in the world-wide revolt of the "masses" today and the winning or seizing of power by those whose comparable lot in other periods of history gave them no real voice in the determination of affairs, no adequate share of the liberties and amenities of "civilization", no worthy recognition of their status as persons. At some of the highest peaks of achievement in the "Christian" civilization of the West there has hitherto been failure at a point most germane to the Christian revelation of life's meaning and purpose. The common man has had least consideration. The "blessings of civilization" have too often been enjoyed at his expense. The "common people" have not come into their kingdom. Now mere revolt is no sign that this flaw in the history of society is being remedied. The rebellion of the victims of a social defect is something different from the repentance of society for its wrongs. If the rebellion merely issues in a transfer of power to those who, having been wronged, care no more than those who have wronged them about the intention of God for society and His demand for moral obedience as well as His gift of abundant life, the result will be no more Christian than the sub-Christian order which it overthrows. It is, nevertheless, possible so to learn from this "revolt of the masses" that society as a whole may mend its ways and offer an obedience to God which will constitute a decisive turning point in the reformation and renewal of civilization. At this point, despite my sober view of the total scene today, I see within the ferment that surrounds us a powerful element that may mark not only the destructive ending of an old era but the creative beginning of a new. Where I find this hope inevitably qualified by grave misgiving is in the fact that at the moment the "common people" seem more likely to ride into their kingdom—or a kingdom of sorts —on the tide of a power even more godless in its standpoint and assumptions than that of older aristocratic tyrannies. If this happens, the final collapse of history's approach to a Christian civilization will only be the more certain. As yet, however, it may not be too late for the lesson to be learned and for an obedient generation to refashion a civilization to which, because of its fuller recognition of the Christian estimate of man—every man —the term "Christian" may be applied with more justification than hitherto.

The second point at which I believe contemporary movements offer us another of the "lessons of history" is to be seen in the part which the coloured races are playing in the ferment of our time—a part which is certain to increase rather than decrease in the stormy era to which we belong. It seems to me that relatively few people in Britain are aware of the magnitude of the revolution now taking place in the balance of power between the white and coloured peoples of the world. We know vaguely that China is "in a bad way", that Japan has suffered a defeat from which the way of recovery will be long. We overhear occasionally that France is having trouble with her colonial possessions in Indo-China and Madagascar. We are aware of the prolonged struggle between the Indonesians and the Netherlands Government. We pride ourselves on a peaceful surrender of British authority in India and Burma though we are a little uneasy about Malaya and about rumblings in various parts of Africa, especially the possible outcome in South Africa of General Smut's supersession by Dr. Malan. But there is all too little awareness that behind these diverse symptoms—even at the heart of a defeated Japan and within a China whose domestic problems are more than enough for statesmanship—there is yet another "rising" of enormous dimensions. It is in part the manifestation within the coloured races of that same revolt of the masses to which I have referred, but it is even more an assertion by the Asiatic and African peoples of their own consciousness of growing strength over against the declining prestige of the West. Most powerfully of all it is a colour-conscious protest against that racial discrimination which has been so marked a feature of much of western civilization during what we too complacently assumed to be its successful periods.

It is not the purpose of this book to discuss that great complex of problems which make up "the colour question". My sole concern in making this reference is to emphasize the fact that amongst the great forces contributing to the restless and precarious character of this age is a movement which arises from another of the fatal weaknesses of what has hitherto been called "Christian civilization". That civilization has, in its modern periods, either established itself on the subordination of the coloured races or it has largely left them out of account. Once more, the revolt of the wronged does not necessarily mean that right will be accomplished, but again it is just possible that it may not be too late for a reformation in world-community which will result in a civilization that transcends racial differences and for this reason also becomes more entitled than its predecessors to the appellation "Christian".

In the preceding pages I have admittedly been dealing with issues which require for their competent handling a range of knowledge and depth of understanding which are beyond my power to command. A Christian Philosophy of History is needed to do full justice to such questions as those which I have touched upon, and not even Professor Toynbee has yet accomplished this. All I have been attempting here is to testify how a non-specialist in these matters can, with the biblical standpoint as his guide, at least begin to see reason in the processes of history. From this standpoint I know that to be able to give a meaning to history depends not on being able to feel that all is going well or that peace and prosperity will come soon; it turns on our being able to see events— "happy" or otherwise—as the outcome of obedience or disobedience to the revealed will of God. Again, from this biblical standpoint I can contemplate the worst as happening in history and yet to some extent see why it happens and do so in the sure conviction that the last word—a redeeming word—lies with God, the Lord of eternity as well as time. Finally, from the biblical standpoint, whether illustrated in the Hebrew prophets or in Jesus Himself, I find it possible to see in contemporary events judgments on the course of history hitherto, lessons from which we may learn and obey. None of this may make life any easier. It may be even less conducive to optimism than some other approaches to life and to history. But it nevertheless makes our days purposive and more than ever responsible. It sets them in a context which gives them greatness. In all this I find spiritual peace, though I know that this peace is given to be the foundation of responsible living, not as an anodyne of care.

From many points of view this is a bad time in which to be alive—a hard, sad and exhausting time. With all its accomplishments and acquisitions of power, this age seems to me, so far as God's good purpose for mankind is concerned, to be one of those "thwarting" periods to which I have referred. The next great age of constructive, generous and fearless living waits on a world-wide mood of penitence, of humble and reverent seeking for the will of God, and unselfish corporate obedience. Whether this will come, or whether greater darkness will follow our unchristian ways, none of us can prophesy. What matters is that we should see the central issue that is at stake and set our personal lives in the way of obedience. In so doing, whether our immediate lot proves pleasant or safe or prosperous is a secondary consideration. If, so far as in us lies, we have made knowledge of God and obedience to His will the chief end of living, we shall have played that part in the history of our time for which we were born and we can leave its vindication and completion to eternity.

(III)

In this discussion of the meaning of history I have had in mind that phrase of George Eliot's which I have already quoted—"the invasion of our private lives by the larger destinies of mankind". I have been thinking of that inextricable entangling of our individual pilgrimage with the corporate history of our age, our race, our nation. Here I accept to the full that Christian rediscovery of the social nature of man which is a characteristic emphasis of our time, though it is nowhere more powerfully expressed than in the New Testament. This recovery of our Christian awareness that the individual is spiritually involved in the fortunes (and the salvation) of the community is another of the points at which contemporary thought, even under the stress of disastrous events, is providentially (I use the word deliberately) applying its corrective to some earlier "Christian" assumptions. We are scarcely likely to see a return to the excessive individualism which marked much religious thought and practice during the last century. And yet, as with so many new or recovered emphases in our Christian thinking, the new is intended to correct the old by supplementing and completing it. It does not necessarily replace or destroy the old. We are members one of another; the true nature of man is social. Life in the Kingdom is life in community—fellowship. Yet at the heart of the mystery of human personality there is individuality, personal identity, and the Christian doctrine of society does not abolish the fact of personal and individual responsibility. I believe that for our full Christian obedience there must be the completest possible "integration" of the individual in the redeemed society (or the society that is in course of redemption); but it seems to me that one of the authentic marks of a Christian society is that in this process of integration the individual does not lose himself in the mass; he so finds himself in the family of God that he is free to be himself, strong enough to make his own distinctive contribution to the common life and sure at the last of a Father's individual care. Here we need for our fullest assurance something more than faith in history or a reasonable ground for believing that events in general are set within an eternal purpose. For each of us there come the great crises of character and fortune in which we know a final solitariness which is not invaded even by the most intimate and sacred of our social relationships. It is then that we need a very personal confidence in a very personal destiny. Generalizations about the outcome of history need to give place to something immediate and particular about our personal encounter with the eternal mysteries—sin, remorse, forgiveness, the ineluctable facts of death and the life to come. Here more than anywhere else it is in a biblical faith that I find my anchorage and spiritual peace. I know no other book or set of books which can be compared to the Bible in its power to speak with intimacy and directness and authority to man in his final privacy as an individual. The secret of it takes us back to that biblical characteristic of which I have already spoken—its powerful presentation of God as a Person concerned with persons. Writers vastly different in their outlook, qualities and opinions, separated from one another by centuries, all write under the sway of an immediate sense of the personal presence of God.

For these writers the creation of the world was not a generalized impersonal process. It was the activity of a personal God, with an individual intention concerning man—man as a person, not as a part of humanity. With all that the Bible says about the rise and fall of nations, the peculiar destiny of Israel, the creation of a redeemed community, it never ceases to speak in personal terms. Always the key-points in its presentation of history appear in the decisive contact between God and a named individual. Progress or regression in regard to the ultimate purposes of God for mankind turn just as decisively on the obedience or disobedience of a particular character. And the culmination of it all is in the Bible's presentation of God's supreme disclosure of himself in the Person of Jesus whose revealing and saving work, though it is

manifestly for "the world", centres itself from beginning
to end on this named person and that.

At this point the Bible leads me to a conclusion about
history which would be the height of egotism if it were
self-engendered or not kept within the awe and humility
which constant reference to Christ evokes. For the cul-
minating revelation of the significance of persons which
we find in Jesus demonstrates, in almost frightening fashion, that the epoch-making moments in the dealings of a
Personal God with persons may occur just as frequently
in relation to any very "ordinary" man or woman as in
connection with those who, on most human reckonings,
would be most likely to fulfil an "historic" rôle in life.
The New Testament is full of incidents which have become historic not because of the native genius or eminent
position of the man, woman or child involved, but because
Christ found it natural to make His contact with such
people the occasion of a revealing word whose power can
never die, or to use their obedience as a turning point in history. Because some of these are named in the New Testament in connection with Christ their names have become
imperishable. But some of them are recorded anonymously
--"a certain man", "a woman in the city". It might have
been anybody. And it is these anybodies who matter.

"The larger destinies of mankind" have very much
"invaded our private lives" in this, our own time. But not
even amidst the mammoth pressures which impersonal
history exercises upon my life today, can I escape the
biblical conclusion that even my "private life", when it
has been forgotten here, will remain historically significant in the sight of God and in the fulfilment of His
purpose.

CHAPTER FOUR

FELLOWSHIP OF GRACE

I SUPPOSE that one whose professional life is bound up with the work of the Church is at a disadvantage when he tries to testify to the influence of the Church in his spiritual pilgrimage. He will be thought of as having a vested interest in what he is commending. I cannot free what I write in this chapter from this limitation, but three observations are relevant here. First, the beginnings of my debt to the Church and its means of grace cover many years during which I had not the slightest idea that my vocation would lie in the Christian ministry. Secondly, it so happens that the course of my ministry has given me an unusually wide and intimate "inside knowledge" of the Church's institutional life and problems. While this has carried with it peculiar advantages for which I shall always feel indebted, it has inevitably meant that I am more aware than most people—even my brethren in the ministry generally—of weaknesses and failures within the life of the Church itself. Yet in complete sincerity I testify that the total result of my wider and more intimate knowledge adds to the gratitude and conviction with which I speak of the Church. Thirdly, although the Church is the setting of my "profession" and the sphere of my "vocation", its most powerful claim upon my life remains in its ability to speak to my deepest and most persistent personal needs. I have many times wished that my ministry was not a "professional" one. No less frequently I have wished that, with full obedience to my sense of vocation, I could be elsewhere than in the

Church's ministry. But never have I felt that I could cease to be a regular and grateful recipient of the Church's ministrations. It is both a privilege and an act of vocational obedience that takes me into the pulpit. It is a profound personal spiritual necessity that takes me into the pew and makes me more at home there than anywhere else.

This attitude is far from being an uncritical one. A sense of freedom to criticize the Church's ways and even to sleep through its ministrations belongs to my earliest understanding of Christian liberty, and as the years have passed I have known good reason to exercise the first, and much temptation to exercise the second, of these elemental freedoms. The discipline of Church attendance was part of that upbringing for which I have already expressed my gratitude. And in view of the common assumption nowadays, reinforced by many biographers and autobiographers, that premature—especially compulsory—Church attendance is one of the surest ways of producing unbelief or spiritual sterility, I take this opportunity of renewing my testimony to what I owe to this phase of my religious education.

It must have been evident to us from our very early years as children that attendance at public worship was something eagerly prized by our parents. If any folk had good cause not to bestir themselves on Sunday morning it was surely my mother and father. The shop (a sweet shop), open until ten and eleven at night from Monday to Friday, closed a few minutes before midnight on Saturday—and, strange as it may now seem, customers would have been available beyond that hour if we had chosen to serve them. Incidentally, Sunday could have been the most profitable day of the week had not my father's convictions ruled out any thought of trading after midnight on Saturday. How tired my parents must have been at this stage of the week, I can only guess. Although we all took it for granted that we should take our share of the chores, business and domestic, an enormous responsibility was carried by the older folk and their work was incessant.

At the time of which I am now speaking eight children, three or four of them still of school age, were living in the little home "over the shop", and the fact that, in addition to countless other responsibilities, my mother made and kept our clothes in repair and my father mended our shoes, illustrates the kind of life they lived. The week's activities, domestic and business, reached a climax on Saturday night and I only had a vague idea of the early morning hour at which rest became possible for our parents. Yet, week after week, year after year, the family pew was fully occupied at morning service on Sunday —mother at one end, father at the other; and to all our recollection, though we have gone different ways, this morning worship was the first main item in the most delightful day of the week. The day was accompanied by various Sabbatarian restrictions. Music had to be "sacred" (though when disputes arose judgment was usually given with a leaning to mercy); books not too light, and no games. Candour requires me to add that there were certain compensations provided, especially the "Sunday Chocolate Box" in which the week's "throwouts" were put—bruised but still succulent. But the essential meaning of the day lay neither in its restrictions nor indulgences. It was in the whole tone of things— a mingling of restfulness and gaiety, of good friendships and rich family life, with a central thread of reverence and thanksgiving. It was the day of the week to look forward to with eagerness and look back upon with content. It was at once a Sabbath and a Day of Resurrection, restful and creative. And at morning and evening there was public worship.

It is scarcely possible to recall with precision what the exercises of public worship meant to a child. I think there is no doubt that amongst the influences that were to endure and to play an increasing part in my spiritual development, the sound of hymn-singing came first. I am sure that "children's hymns" contributed very little to this experience. The power of which I became conscious at a very early age was not dependent on rhyming morality simplified to a child's intellect; still less did it reside in juvenile melodies specially written by adults to meet their measure of a youngster's musical intelligence. The revealing moments were nearly all associated with the classic hymns of the Church, whose majestic rhythm, serene harmonies and words only dimly understood, added to the glories of this mysterious universe and caused me to lift up my heart. Ever since those days a really great hymn has steadied my spirit and reinforced my faith as nothing else can do. Again and again, out of tiredness, frustration, humiliation or doubt I have been lifted by this most catholic element in the Church's worship to the point where I have known afresh that even if I could not understand God I could glorify Him and enjoy Him for ever. I may add that one result of this has been a constant stirring of my indignation against all those responsible for public worship who treat carelessly this part of their ministry and allow a service to be disfigured by hymns that are banal, wishy-washy or otherwise undeserving of a place in a dignified act of praise. Few things have surprised me more during recent years, in which I have had the opportunity of worship in the churches of many denominations, than my discovery of the great disservice which is being rendered to the Church (and to the souls of men) by carelessness or indifference in this matter.

A second powerful influence which began to operate at an early age is bound up with the voice of preachers, both in the reading of Scripture and in the sermons. In both instances the language used was more often than not beyond a child's comprehension. Comparatively few passages in the Bible are entirely within the compass of a very young mind and I am not convinced that to simplify them—especially to turn them (as I have sometimes heard done) into a kind of chatty paraphrase of the original—is to serve the greatest purpose which the public reading of Scripture in an act of worship is meant to fulfil. (Of course I recognize the place of this simplification for certain instructional purposes.) I believe that long before full understanding of their content is possible, innumerable passages of Scripture can, through public reading, yield up something of their beauty, dignity and spiritual power, especially if they are read by one for whom the reading is worship. The resulting influence is more than cultural and it may be different from instructional, but it can contribute powerfully towards growth in spiritual sensitiveness and insight.

As for my childhood's listening to sermons, can I pretend that I enjoyed them ? Never, in the sense that I enjoyed a good tale or good music. Yet it is a doubtful approach to the mystery of preaching to measure it by its entertainment value, whether for childhood or age. A sermon is truth becoming alive in personality, and if, for a moment only, the life—the *living* Word—is seen and the authentic fire felt, then the miracle of grace is enacted. It was in my 'teens that the *content* of preaching, as proclamation, exposition, argument or appeal became real to me; but long before this stage was reached, as I learned the art of sitting still and "all sorts of funny things" went "round my head", I would suddenly catch sight of an earnest face in the pulpit; I would find my wandering attention caught by a phrase or by the tone of voice used; and at least I would become dimly aware that high issues were at stake and that the man of God was engaged in a greater exercise than talking. As for the rest of his discourse, if sometimes nature withstood grace and I soundly slept, invariably I would wake up to find my father's arm around me and hear a noble organ note summoning me to praise. And that, I think, is spiritually true of what has happened to me many times since.

I have dwelt on this childhood's introduction to a faith created and nurtured in worship, chiefly because it is an essential part of the testimony which I am making, and also because it has important implications for Christian parents. If, for example, we had merely been packed off to Sunday School by tired elders who were yielding to some familiar plausibilities for not attending public worship themselves, it is difficult to imagine that our education in spiritual things would have been the same. What we could not help knowing was that this business of Church-going really mattered to people who might well have been doing something else. A sense of caring about this thing and of great sincerity in the exercise were unmistakable. Again, these older folk were—or, at any rate, my father was—no more uncritical of the Church's ministrations than his children became. At home we discussed such time-honoured weaknesses as the frailties of the choir, the little pomposities of church officers, the mannerisms of preachers and all the rest of it, with freedom, hilarity or indignation. As I have already indicated, subsequent years have provided me with more than enough raw material on which to exercise the same emotions. But it never occurred to us that these things—or even graver causes for criticism in the inconsistencies of professing Christians and the Church's failures as judged by its own Gospel—should result in our abandoning the habit of public worship. Nor could we conclude that they made any difference to our need to offer thanks and praise to God, to bring our personal confessions and aspirations to the place where the Gospel was proclaimed and where prayer could most fittingly be offered. A phrase of William Penn's expresses what I have always felt to be a right attitude to the blemishes and failures of the Church: "They have a right to censure that have a heart to help." This does not mean that the ultimate authority and grace of the Church are derived from the support we give it. That assumption belongs to pride and folly as well as to a mistaken view of the Church. But where the discipleship of its members, the calling of its ministers or the wisdom of its councils are impaired by failure or sin, our highest obligation is to renew our own obedience to Him who "loved the Church and gave Himself for it, that He might present it to Himself a glorious Church, not having spot or wrinkle or any such thing, but that it should be holy and without blemish".

I think this attitude has something to do with the fact that through years in which I have been more aware than in earlier days of the weakness of "institutional Christianity", the Church's hold on me has grown. And it has done so through periods in which I have been conscious —both in the world about me and in my own experience —of life's sharpest challenges to the validity of the Christian faith. The point is that the tensions, the wrestling with misgivings, the struggle against wrong, the search for truth, have all been dealt with from within a fellowship which, with all its weaknesses and disloyalties, has carried within itself the secret of its own reformation as well as that of the world's redemption. To stand aloof from it is not merely to stand outside its disorders; it is to remove ourselves from its springs of spiritual power and to deprive our own souls of regular, disciplined acknowledgment of the truth as it is in Christ—truth of which the Church's very existence is an explicit avowal and proclamation. For me, it has been through this constant return and re-committal to the life of the Church, being as sincere in my criticism as in my confession of personal need, that there has again and again been borne in upon my heart and mind the truth of the Christian Gospel and the reality of its power to save.

In this testimony to the place of the Church in the maintenance of my own faith—or of the Faith's hold on me—I find my debt gathering around three principal means of grace. The first is associated with worship, the expression of one of the oldest and deepest of all our instincts. Worship may find expression, of course, in innumerable ways other than those of the Church's acts of worship. All of us are constantly worshipping—some one or some thing, some ideal or ambition or object of desire. Human nature's capacity to give itself, to "let itself go" in aspiration, longing, or enthusiastic application to a particular end—all this is worship. The trouble with our age is not that it has ceased to worship—men can no more do that than they can dispense with breathing; it is that the objects of worship have been inadequate, unworthy or so diverse that there has been no central commanding loyalty providing both full release for our capacity to worship and the corrective to wrong conceptions of what is truly worshipful. For me the Christian life begins with acknowledgment of the fact that there is only one object "at all times worthy of worship and wonder". It is the God and Father of our Lord Jesus Christ and our Father. This Object is both all-embracing and unifying. Everything worth loving, worth waxing enthusiastic about, worth surrendering our souls to, worth living for and dying for, comes from Him. All truth, beauty and goodness are there and the key to His nature and its manifold riches is in the Person of Jesus Christ.

True worship cannot be restricted to particular times and places or to conventional "acts of worship" as provided by the Church. All Christian discipleship is Christian worship, all life our liturgy. But to fulfil such a claim as this and to keep the crucial fact of Christ central to life's manifold interests and activities, I find it imperative to keep those regulated pauses in the normal business of living for which the Church provides in its acts of worship. Here, central to all else, are the lifting-up of Christ and the proclamation of the Gospel in praise and prayer, in the reading of Scripture, the preaching of the Word and the administration of the Sacraments. I can find fault with the way in which these things are done. I can own preferences for this element and that in the "diet" of worship. I can acknowledge periods and moods in which I have "not felt like it" or have seriously questioned (as I still do) the essential relevance of some ways of worship to a fully Christian understanding of the nature of God and the claims of our discipleship. I want to see and feel a more creative, dynamic element in Christian worship than is apparent in much that takes place in churches. But none of these things alters my persistent need for the moment, regularly renewed, when, through the best ministrations which the Church can at present provide, I bring my mind afresh to the truth as it is in Christ, I offer my obedience to the will of God revealed in him,

I submit my spirit to His Holy Spirit and lift up my heart in adoration and praise.

I would stress two aspects of this activity—worship—which for me are essential to it. They are adoration and personal submission.

Emotional and aesthetic factors inevitably enter into the first of these—or, at any rate, into the form which our act of adoration takes. In one sense I can say that I have never found the Church's acts of worship adequate to my impulse to adore. In another sense I can testify that there is always some point at which the worship of the Church enables me to offer my heart's devotion. The circumstances of my calling in recent years have given me the opportunity to engage in many different forms of worship. I have sat with painted fuzzy-wuzzies in New Guinea as they have tapped out strange drum rhythms and glorified God in fearful and wonderful fashion. I have followed Indian lyrics set to melodic lines fundamentally different from any western musical forms. I have been washed by waves of sound in American auditoriums while mighty organs with (seemingly) permanent *tremolo* stops and vesper-bell attachments have expressed something that somebody wanted to say. I have been sobered by the austerities of Reformed worship in Geneva, and have sung chorales in Lutheran churches in Germany and Sweden. The calm of Friends' Meeting Houses has eased my mind, and trumpets have roused me as I have joined Africans in praise in the Belgian Congo. In College Chapels and Anglican parish churches I have seen jubilation mixed with discretion and in Cathedrals I have listened with worshipping sympathy while choral and liturgical experts have offered our oblation. Most familiarly of all, I have lifted up my heart in the Methodist churches of my youth and the Congregational churches in which my membership and ministry are rooted. In all this I have been conscious of a twofold reaction in my own mind and spirit. There has been an element of detachment coupled with a quality of deep and absolute committal. By detachment I mean that my mind has seldom ceased to be conscious of the limited extent to which even the most nobly devised act of worship "says" what ought to be said. Sometimes the mood has been "What *does* God think of this?"; sometimes, amidst much that satisfies, it has been "Not even this can say it". And yet, with this undercurrent of awareness that the best we can offer is never good enough or true enough, my heart has been at one with the central meaning of the act and I have rejoiced to affirm again and again and through various means of expression that "I believe in God the Father Almighty, maker of heaven and earth. And in Jesus Christ His only Son our Lord" . . . and that "Therefore with angels and archangels, and with all the company of heaven, we laud and magnify Thy glorious name, evermore praising Thee and saying: Holy, holy, holy, Lord God of hosts; heaven and earth are full of Thy glory: glory be to Thee, O Lord, most high."

It belongs to the nature of adoration that we make our offering and lift up our hearts without thought that in this act we ourselves shall derive some benefit from it. And yet, since I am testifying to those things which have kept and nurtured me in the faith, I cannot ignore the fact that in renewing my affirmation of belief and offering praise where it is due there has come into my own life great spiritual reinforcement. Nothing can shake my conviction that in such moments I have been in the real Presence of God, and have known for myself that which was from the beginning, that which is and ever shall be, world without end.

I have called the second aspect of worship "submission". In some respects this is a weaker and less dignified word than I want to employ for my purpose, yet I use it in the serious conviction that there is a critical point in our spiritual life at which the greatest things remain hidden from us unless we realize that we *are* weak and have no dignity of our own worth standing upon. This truth is not incompatible with a proper self-reliance, self-respect and independence of character in all the ordinary business of living. Still less does it conflict with that greater strength and serenity of bearing which Jeremy Taylor called "my dignity as a Christian". It springs from what I have just been saying about adoration. It begins with the realization that in the God and Father of our Lord Jesus Christ there is One "worthy at all times to be sung with undefiled tongue", and it follows from the knowledge that in such a Presence the inevitable attitude for man is upon his knees. There are many commonly accepted standards (good ones, too) judged by which we can hold up our heads, assert ourselves, and all the rest of it; but in Christ there is a standard of righteousness, a revelation, of truth, a disclosure of the meaning of holiness, of the consequences of sin and the depths of the divine mercy, judged by which we can only bow in unforced humility of mind and heart. And I believe that it is at this point of inmost "yielding", most naturally reached in worship, that the eternal, living reality of God makes its most powerful impact upon our souls.

For myself, I find another aspect of Christian discipleship associated with this submissive core of worship. It is at the moment when we acknowledge the supremely worshipful nature of God that personal decisions are most naturally made in regard to Christian obedience in conduct. There have been major crises in my life when the

decision has been—for me—of epoch-making importance. One occurred soon after I left my original home in
1915 for army service and discovered that not even
the richest spiritual inheritance is in itself a sufficient
foundation for Christian living. There must be a personal
and responsible appropriation of the grace and truth to
which the inheritance testifies. Others have occurred at
turning-points in my vocational insight and obedience.
Still others have accompanied the most inward personal
crises of all, as when bereavement has suddenly altered
the complexion of the universe, or the discovery of what
my heart is capable of has proved for me the truth of
Richard Baxter's words that "a holy calling will not save
an unholy man". At nearly all such moments, awareness
in worship of the grace and truth that are in Jesus Christ
has not only constrained me to bow in spirit before Him;
it has clearly required me to assent in conduct to some
implication of the truth so revealed. And repeatedly I
have learned that to stop short of this element in submission—to withhold the moral obedience that issues in
more selfless service—is to quench the Spirit and block
the channels of power. Conversely, I have known that
practical obedience at this point is a step in the revealing
process, a way of access to spiritual power and the deepening of conviction. It is the point at which, in matters small
and great, we learn the validity of that spiritual law: "If
any man willeth to do His will, he shall know of the teaching, whether it be of God."

I am more concerned in this book to make my positive
testimony to the way in which the Faith has kept its hold
on me than to speculate about the reasons for its loosening
hold on others, but I must here affirm my deep conviction about the relation between the possession of a living
faith and regular recourse to the means of grace accessible

in the Church's worship. It is an essential part of my belief—as I have already indicated—that, by the goodness of God, the means of grace are many and varied and are not confined to ecclesiastical channels. I can speak with sincerity about worshipping in the open-air in spirit and in truth, about seeing the heavens opened in a concert performance of Bach's *B Minor Mass* or Handel's *Messiah*, or being taken nearer to Calvary by the Bach Choir's performance of the *St. Matthew Passion* than through a feeble "rendering" of Stainer's *Crucifixion* by an indifferent Church choir. I know something about the "sacraments of the common life" and I don't take it too unkindly when I am urged to fold to my heart my brother, substituting smiles for hymns and kindly deeds for prayers until the wide earth "shall *seem* our Father's temple". Yet I know full well that if I had relied on these extra-ecclesiastical means of grace alone to carry me through the last thirty years, my spiritual anchorage would have been insecure. I speak with some knowledge on this matter. At a critical point in my spiritual development, when the possession of a more first-hand consciousness of God was my most urgent need, it was not by folding to my heart some of my brother Tommies in the army that I learned more about God. In so far as the metaphors of affection are appropriate to what happened, it was as I knelt in Church and felt Christ fold me to His heart that revelation came—a revelation in the light of which I knew something stronger and more hopeful about my fellow men and my duty towards them.

It happens that of my twenty-six years in the ministry twelve have been spent in work which has left the practice of Church attendance very largely optional for me rather than obligatory, and I have sometimes reasoned with myself that as a relief from fairly exacting professional responsibilities towards many churches, my most appropriate sabbath-keeping would be in non-ecclesiastical exercises and recreations. But I confess that if I have yielded to this for more than an occasional physical restorative I have soon begun to feel much weaker spiritually, and I believe I have then become less clear in Christian insight. I am quite ready to recognize in this the operation of personal factors from which it may be unwise to draw conclusions for general application. But I have talked much with men and women who, genuinely mourning their own loss of Christian conviction and spiritual peace during the last decade or so, have obviously been trying to remedy their condition without having at hand anything like fresh supplies of the medicine most needed.

For years they have either kept away from the Church altogether, or they have made but hesitant, intermittent contacts with it in circumstances which have mainly provided them with grounds for contending that the Church is no longer what it was or what it ought to be. But their real trouble—or a large part of it—has been that unfamiliarity with the means of grace, prolonged disuse of those instruments of Christian learning which the Church's acts of worship provide, has resulted in something comparable to a lapse into illiteracy on the part of people, who, having once learned to read, have maintained no occasions for exercising their faculty. I say this with deep sympathy and concern for such people and without any abatement of my desire to see the Church so truly reformed by its own Gospel that it will minister more powerfully and less ambiguously to contemporary need; but I see little likelihood that such men and women as I have described will find the way back to a vital faith, or the way forward to a richer spiritual life than they once knew, by experimenting with all other means of grace and leaving the Church's ministrations unheeded.

I have put Worship first amongst the three principal means of grace for which I am indebted to the Church. My second acknowledgment gathers around the word Fellowship. This has been a hard-worked word in recent years and in some of its uses it has been weakened and sentimentalized until it has become less profound in its significance than any Christian term should be. Christian fellowship is not just a getting-together on an easy basis for comparatively trivial ends and relying on amiability to solve all problems in human relationships. It is not even this plus a kind of religious post-script. It is the drawing of men and women into the knowledge of one another because they are first drawn to the "light of the knowledge of the glory of God in the face of Jesus Christ". The chief end of their coming together is God's glory. Worshipping together, they also learn together the meaning of Christian obedience. They express their obedience corporately as well as individually and they find its determining principles, as well as the basis of their own relationships to one another, in the Cross of Christ and the power of His resurrection. It is in these terms that I use the word Fellowship and testify to my own experience of it and my debt to the Church through which I have known it. Here it will be convenient to speak of three aspects of the experience as I have known them, first, in the fellowship of the local church, secondly, in that of the Church throughout the world, and, thirdly, in consciousness of the Communion of Saints.

My life has been extraordinarily rich in friendships and in countless personal contacts which, though too fleeting to be the basis of fully developed human relationships, have, nevertheless, been significant and taught me more of life's depth and greatness. Many of these have, of course, arisen as a result of my calling and I cannot argue, from a somewhat specialized experience and opportunity, that what has constituted for me so rich a means of grace is in the same way accessible to others. Yet, again, I begin where for me the whole process began, at an open door to Christian fellowship which *is* available to all and sundry—the door of a very average local church, within which a good share of the Church's imperfections and infidelities to its own Gospel were to be found.

I did not know at first hand the original Wesley Chapel in which my father was converted but there was one feature of its life which is relevant to my own testimony here. At the time of his conversion my father was already a political radical and for the rest of his days he found in the Christian Gospel and the Christian doctrine of man ground for the persistent left-ward move of his social and political convictions. Yet he was converted in a church in which class distinctions were most glaringly illustrated by rigidly separated and partitioned pews for rich and poor. The "poor seats" remained his throughout his association with the church. Even at a later date, in the church of my own childhood, there was a part of the building, with separate access and comfortable upholstery, familiarly known as the House of Lords, into which I never entered except as part of a childish escapade out of worshipping hours. In both churches the Methodist Class Meeting was a vigorous part of the membership's corporate life and through the greater number of my father's years in these meetings his class-leaders were poles asunder from him politically. There is food for reflection in the fact that, in spite of these contrasts between views held persistently by my father and those most obviously prevailing in the Church, it was the

Church which provided the channel through which the converting power came; but I recall this situation for another reason. Despite the subsequent strengthening of his radical views and the increasing seriousness of his political controversy with opponents (he was quick-tempered in these matters, with good reason in his personal history to feel strongly about social injustices) he found himself drawn closer and closer, within the fellowship of the Church, to those from whom he differed most seriously. Those separated seats were not the whole story of the Church's contribution to the problem of human relationships, nor was the Methodist Class Meeting a hypocrisy. Often against inclination and will, men and women of gravely divergent views and vastly different backgrounds, were brought together through their service to the Church and their common worship in ways that compelled some consideration of the meaning of their differences in the light of Christ. This was not without its effect upon their knowledge of the points of difference, or on the subsequent development of their opinions; but its greatest effect was in the sphere of personal relationships—in the spiritual compulsion to think differently about and care more for, the kind of people of whom they would otherwise have only an impersonal knowledge or whom they would meet only on a plane where the deepest encounters between person and person never take place.

This has remained for me one of the most exciting aspects of Christian fellowship. The local situation has varied from time to time but there has been no place in life—except my home—at which I have known human relationships at a depth comparable to that of the local Church's fellowship. There, relationships have been forged which no change of place can weaken and which have been more than humanly satisfying; they have been revealing. And I most emphatically include in this assertion not only the friendships which have been made easy through congenial tastes and natural sympathies but those relationships to which the term "friendship" in its natural usage would scarcely apply. Some of these have been the occasion of the most costly personal encounters I have ever known; they have been accompanied by much tension of mind and stress of spirit. For the most part the discipline has led me—and, I hope, the other parties to the encounter !—to a far deeper understanding of the human heart (my own as well as other people's) and the result has been enrichment of fellowship. In some few other cases an element of unresolved tension has remained, yet throughout the entire range of these relationships my sense of caring for people—for all sorts and conditions of men—has grown and one of the most convincing arguments for the worth-whileness of life that I have ever experienced is bound up with this gift of grace which has come my way through the local fellowship of the Church. This is one of the points at which the hazards and agonizing accompaniments of a second world war have deepened my faith rather than weakened it. For, through the sharing of harder questions and deeper sorrows, so many of these relationships have not merely endured; they have stood out more clearly in their own impregnable right as witness to the things which cannot be shaken. This does not in itself justify wars or any other villainous consequences of sin; but it points to other elements in life than the wayward doings of our generation, elements which have to be taken into account in arriving at a verdict on the ultimate meaning of things.

Much of the richness of this local fellowship of the Church, as I have known it, is related to the world-wide scope of the Christian fellowship. Here, again, I have been specially privileged in the large extent to which I have enjoyed, at first hand, some knowledge of the world out-reach of the Church. While it is proper to testify to this and to take into account the particular advantages which lie behind my judgments on this quality in the Church's life, I may, nevertheless, point out again that more extensive knowledge also provides a wider range of data concerning the weaknesses of the Church. I recall the sudden chilling of my spirit when I first met, within the life of a very young "Younger Church", marks of that tired mood of frustration and failure which has so often come upon older churches in a Western Christendom where the Good News has lost its freshness. "I regret to say," publicly reported an Indian minister to me at an annual meeting of his congregation, "that during the last year there has been no improvement in Church members." This way of putting it was a slight misuse of English in an endeavour to say that no new members had been received during the year; but I think he was speaking better than he knew and unconsciously explaining the lack of numerical progress. "The trouble with this Church," declaimed another Indian minister in my hearing, "is that there are no surprises in it." He might have been speaking at the end of a long ministry in western suburbia; he was, in fact, commenting on the spiritual inertia of a young congregation in South India. I have seen much, besides such symptoms as these, which proves that even a younger church can become withered in a generation.

But this is only a small part of the story. What I have known to be far more significant is that in country after country, amongst people at infinitely varied stages of cultural development, I have seen the authentic marks of

Christian fellowship, gathering around a central loyalty which transcends differences of race, nationality, language or cultural inheritance. I have seen worship conducted in many tongues and with unfamiliar rites, but through strange language and form I have been more conscious of its central familiarity than anything else. I have discussed questions of personal character and social behaviour with a group of deacons in New Guinea, one of whom as a child had played about the outskirts of the cannibal feast following the murder of James Chalmers and Oliver Tomkins. I have been in consultation with Indian Christian leaders who could bring to bear upon their judgments the riches of a great and ancient culture. In these and innumerable other contacts, as vividly varied in their local characteristics, the most distinctive mark has been that the standard of reference in discussing questions of conduct and shaping personal loyalty has been one and the same Lord. And the sense of being deeply at home with all such groups was mine because of the unmistakable presence of one and the same Spirit. Since the end of the second world war I have been in council with leaders of younger Churches whose Christian strength and fidelity had recently been put to the test of bitter persecution, torture and the threat of death. From these I have heard personal testimony, as old as the New Testament, as new as today, of a grace sufficient to such tests as these. They have talked with me of others of their race who were not spared from death but who died as more than conquerors in the power of the same Lord. To fellow-Christians in twenty different countries which I have visited in recent years I have been able to say, across all the differences, "Now, therefore, we are no more strangers and foreigners, but fellow-citizens with the saints and of the household of God; and are built upon the foundation of the apostles and prophets, Jesus Christ Himself being the chief corner-stone."

Although my unusual opportunities have made specially vivid this fact of Christian fellowship reaching across the frontiers, some experience of its essential meaning is not dependent on particular advantages. There are few local Churches in the west which are without a personal link with some part of the Church overseas, and through the missionary societies or the central machinery of the denominations there are powerful channels through which the local Church may not only fulfil its world-wide obedience but may receive richly from other parts of the "holy church throughout all the world". The number, variety and strength of these links reminding the local fellowship of its world-wide out-reach are greater today than they have ever been, and in a world where divisiveness shows little sign of diminishing, this great fact in the Church's life is of greater significance than ever. Not least amongst its contributions to the spiritual need of this generation is the proof which it has given of profoundly real Christian fellowship uniting men and women even across the frontiers of war. In this matter, again, my work has happened to give me special advantages. In the service of the International Missionary Council I have been personally involved in that liaison work through which the common responsibilities of Churches on both sides of the war-frontiers were maintained during wartime in the name of one international body. Personal contacts have brought home to me, in the most moving way, the fact that behind the administration of such international services there has been a large body of men and women, "enemies" to one another in terms of their national status, but keeping alive in thought and prayer those relationships with one another in Christ which,

even in this world, give us a supranational citizenship
and command us by a supranational loyalty.

This book is not an account of what is nowadays called
the Ecumenical Movement, but in testifying to the experiences through which I have found spiritual sustenance
and true means of grace I must acknowledge my debt of
gratitude for the high privilege of receiving so much at
first hand from this manifold, "ecumenical" life of the
Christian fellowship. I have known it at sufficiently close
quarters to be more cautious than some Christian publi-
cists in making claims about its capabilities for action in
the world today. To talk of "The World Church" as
though there were a solid, undivided international
Christian organization able to deal with power-politicians
in their own terms is misleading factually and spiritually.
Apart from the radical cleavage between Romans and
non-Romans (which shows so little sign of being lessened)
the obstacles to union between the non-Roman Churches
themselves are many and deep. No less difficult is the
achievement through the Churches of something like an
international Christian judgment on contemporary issues.
And yet the fact remains that we are living at a time
through which the Churches everywhere are rapidly
recovering something of the richness of their universal
inheritance and calling and are doing so along lines which
are leading both to a truer "catholicity" than has hitherto
been manifest and a more powerful and united proclamation to the world of the word of Salvation. One of the
chief instruments through which this is taking place
(amongst the non-Roman Churches) is that "ecumenical
movement" which operates mainly through Councils
of Churches, National Christian Councils, the International Missionary Council and the newly-established
World Council of Churches. These are not merely the

preserve of ecumenical specialists; they are expressions of a widespread movement of the Spirit which is disturbing and renewing Churches in every land. The organizational structure of the movement may prove to be relatively short-lived, but the truth and power which are being imparted through it are not likely to be evanescent. It is bringing to Churches everywhere new insights and inspirations concerning a common Christian inheritance richer than that of any one denomination, a sense of a common urgent task as wide as the world, and a consciousness of fellowship which at the deepest level has already transcended racial and national differences. Nowadays I cannot worship in any local Church without realizing that I am at a focusing point of this Church ecumenical; whether in London, New York or on a South Sea Island, I am, in fact, at the centre of things—the things which belong to the world's peace, and at the heart of the supranational family of God. In very rich measure this realization can belong to every worshipper in every local Church as the true nature of the Church is understood.

But, for me, the "ecumenical" character of the Church does not end with its world-wide out-reach. It is something which goes back through history and makes the "living past" a present reality. Further, as part of the same mystery, it reaches out into the life beyond this where "history" is being fulfilled, corrected and redeemed, and where all who are "in Christ" are alive for evermore.

I have spoken in an earlier chapter of "the sense of the past" and have recognized that personal characteristics apparently make it easier for some people than for others to possess a "feeling for history". Yet there is no point at which this can more easily become a common experience, carrying spiritual potency, than in the Church's worship where contemporary acts and speech are so manifestly bound up with the mightiest events of the centuries and the whole drama of Christian history. Still more powerfully, though I fear that the reality and splendour of this thing is far less frequently perceived than it could and should be—at the heart of this act called Worship there is a real entering into a life which transcends these dimensions of time and space, while it also includes them. Nowhere do I feel so convincingly as I do in Christian worship that death has been put in its place, that it remains subservient to the love of God and has been swallowed up in victory. I believe there was a period during R. W. Dale's ministry at Carr's Lane Chapel, Birmingham, when every Sunday morning service opened with the Easter Hymn

Christ the Lord is risen today,
Hallelujah !

The practice may have become liturgically monotonous but I have for a long time felt that this affirmation is the authentic introduction to Christian worship and that from this point all the other miracles proceed, especially the great miracles of fellowship. In the presence of a living Lord our minds and hearts are given power to bridge distances and hold communion with fellow-worshippers in other lands. In the same Presence there is given to mortal men a power to perceive beyond the present and to know by foretaste something of the life of the Communion of Saints. I am well aware that this cannot be put to the proof by tests selected on a basis of unbelief or by minds ignorant of, or out of sympathy with, the great facts of Christian history, the testimony of the Bible and the long-considered verdicts of Christian experience and conviction. I can only testify that, in common with countless men and women throughout the ages and in every part of the world today, I find myself initiated through Christian worship into this high and splendid mystery. Through it I perceive that the past is not dead and that my life is held within a Communion in which the victories which matter most have already been won.

In it I know myself to be one with the ransomed of the Lord who have "come to Zion with songs and everlasting joy upon their heads". Life here may still have some nasty shocks for me and more pain and sorrow than I have yet experienced; but knowing, as I do through Christian worship, what fellowship within the immortalities means, I cannot be fearful about the morrow.

In the preceding chapter I spoke of the term "Church" as supplying, along with the term "Christian civilization", the answer to the great central questions about the meaning of history. In view of what I have written it is probably needless to add that I believe the term "Church" embodies more of the essentials of the answer than does "Christian civilization", even though much of the visible life of the Church is bound up with and dependent upon a Christian civilization. But of the two, it is the Church which explicitly and continuously declares to men that the secret of its own life and of "Christian" civilization is Christ. It is the Church which sets all its activities in a context in which we are made aware of eternity as well as time. It is there more than anywhere else that, while richly experiencing personal fulfilment in social relationships, we realize that at their highest these experiences are only the beginning of a personal life and a corporate destiny going far beyond anything that is possible here. Further, it is from the Church—from its Gospel and through its means of Grace—that there proceed the vision and the power through which "civilization" can both perceive its Christian purpose and attain its Christian character.

Yet these claims concerning the Church can only be made alongside a frank and humble recognition that even the Church carries its treasure in earthen vessels, that these can become as corrupt and un-Christian as an un-Christian civilization, and that its ministers and members can become unfaithful to their calling, in the worship of God, in their personal dedication and their obligation to serve all the world in His saving Name. I have more than once spoken of moments in my experience of the Church, and of my own calling and its fulfilment, when I have been tremblingly aware of this peril. In fact I seldom escape consciousness of the danger even amidst the most impregnable certainties of the Faith. If (often surprisingly to me) its presence does not "shake my Faith" it does remind me again and again where my dependence lies. I know that for the sustenance of the Church, the creation of a Christian civilization and the fulfilment of our destiny, social and personal, we are from beginning to end dependent creatures, children of that "Fatherhood from whom every family in heaven and earth is named", dependent on a Saviour who is both Lord of the Church and Lord of history. In that dependence lies our strength.

CHAPTER FIVE

MIGHTY PURPOSE

"THIS is the true joy of life", says Shaw in the Preface to *Man and Superman*, "the being used for a purpose recognized by yourself as a mighty one ; the being thoroughly worn out before you are thrown on the scrap-heap; the being a force of Nature instead of a feverish, selfish little clod of ailments and grievances complaining that the world will not devote itself to making you happy."

The ideas suggested by being "a force of Nature", with the "scrap-heap" at the end, fall somewhat short of the Christian doctrine of man, but there resounds in this definition of life's true joy a note which is familiar to all who have found vocational contentment through their Christian Faith. If life is really using us to the full and if we know that its use of us arises from a mighty purpose, then however arduous our days may be, deep content of spirit can be ours. On the other hand, a sense of aimlessness concerning the way in which our years are spent, a consciousness of capacities incompletely used, contributes to, as well as arises from, doubt about the essential meaning of things, and one of its most pathetic and most frequent consequences is a complaining spirit; we become "feverish, selfish little clods of ailments and grievances".

Such testimony as I can make to the ways in which life has kept me in the Faith would be very incomplete if it did not include a word about the vocational peace which I have known, and (at least by implication) the reasons for any vocational uneasiness which I may still experience. In using a phrase like "vocational peace" I would make it clear that I think of something quite different from an easy job or an untroubled life. As Shaw recognized, "being thoroughly worn out" may be a necessary part of the experience. Obstinate questionings may return again and again; persistent doubt about one's competence to do a certain job is almost certain to recur. But these things can co-exist with a deep sense of compulsion concerning the rightness of following a particular course, and they can be accompanied by the conviction that the whole business is subject to more than chance or personal whim; it is determined and finally used by a "mighty purpose".

I am well aware that I write this testimony at a time when vocational uncertainty is more widespread than ever and vocational freedom is increasingly curtailed. In what follows I hope it will be clear that I know, by more than hearsay, something of what these things mean. I have no thought of merely telling a personal story of one who has been more fortunate than other people. I want to bear witness to truths about life's use of us which are, I believe, applicable to us all.

Once again I venture to begin my exposition of some general principles by reference to their embodiment in the home of my childhood. The story of an insignificant owner of a little sweet-shop may not, on the face of it, provide the best starting point for affirmations about Christian vocation. I can only say that some of the lessons which I learned through this story—by sight and "feel" even more than by words—have remained an essential part of my understanding of purposive, satisfying Christian living.

My father's life was spent in hard and undistinguished toil—undistinguished, as this word is ordinarily used.

His business operations were slight; they never involved more than the affairs of a small retail shop. He could use his hands well, for he was a more than ordinarily competent amateur carpenter; but the whole of his work as a craftsman was limited to his shop-fitting and the making of home furniture. He loved gardens and possessed "green fingers" but for many years his gardening opportunities were restricted to a small back-yard and window-boxes. Yet within this kind of environment I witnessed a man profoundly convinced that he was called to glorify God. Year after year, decade after decade, the conviction sustained him and gave him joy in very ordinary work. Repeatedly I heard him quote, not with a pietistic accent but as a vigorous life-principle. "Whatsoever ye do, in word or deed, do all in the name of the Lord Jesus, giving thanks to God and the Father by Him." And at the end of a tricky piece of work—perhaps one in which he had succeeded in making a comely and useful article out of scraps of wood; or a shop window-dressing for an Easter or Christmas season—he would stand back from his work for a moment and say with deep sincerity: "Establish Thou the work of our hands upon us; yea, the work of our hands establish Thou it."

Two characteristics were bound up with this attitude. One was an almost fanatical zeal for accuracy in work. If he was making a drawer, it must fit into place like a hand in a glove. The door of a show-case must close with absolute precision. If he was teaching me to drive a nail, saw a piece of wood or wrap and tie a parcel, he would persistently demand impeccable care. Accuracy, cleanness of finish, jobs done to endure—for these things he had literally a religious passion. And the second characteristic was that larger quality of which accuracy is part—integrity. Petty dishonesties, the little subterfuges and sharp practices that so easily attach themselves to small and struggling businesses—these things had for him a kind of nightmare fear. The thought of them seemed to induce an actual physical revulsion. I think one of the lowest Hells to which his imagination could have descended would have been the Black Market of these recent years. For him, failure in integrity was something which cut across the grain of the universe.

Not long since I stood in front of the little shop in which I became aware that a passion for work well done and for integrity in service are marks of a life that is one with God—not the only marks but authentic ones. The scene had greatly changed and I could see little trace of the faithful handiwork of past years. And inevitably I reflected that, far greater than local changes, are the convulsions which have shaken all the world since then, shattering the work of craftsmen of many generations, assailing the assumption that integrity matters, and creating a sense of insecurity that pervades all life today. Yet I do not believe that a mere nostalgic clinging to the lessons of childhood accounts for the conviction, borne in upon me afresh as I stood there, that something in my father's work belongs to the eternities and that wherever men have cared for accuracy and integrity the work of their hands has been established for ever. This conviction is the bedrock of such vocational certainty and peace as I have ever known. Prior to my belief that I have been "called" or "led" in this direction or that, I have known that certain qualities in work have been required of me which arise from the fact that in everything I have done I have been primarily responsible to God—not to the customers whom I first served in the old shop, not to subsequent employers, nor to the State, nor to a body of Church deacons or Church members, not even to an ecumenical committee. Fidelity to these and contentment in their service have followed from this prior calling. In a diversity of "trades, professions, occupations, offices or employments" (to use the old Inland Revenue classification) I have known but one vocation—the "mighty purpose" of glorifying God.

Without any humbug in the matter, I can claim that this has fortified me and given me "true joy in life" at very humdrum and otherwise tiresome levels of service. And since it is so commonly assumed nowadays that millions of people are denied by dulling circumstances that element in spiritual peace which comes from knowledge of "being used", I would say a further word about coping vocationally with an uninspiring environment and routine jobs.

Here I must at once acknowledge that I cannot speak from the inside of that situation which is such a fruitful source of uneasiness and is specially characteristic of our age—the grind of factory life. Its shadow was over the earlier days of my childhood's home and I have never been able to think lightly of the occupational setting which industrialism imposes on the vast mass of my contemporaries. All my social convictions have been in line with that pressure for radical reform which has resulted in enormous changes in our own times and has, in fact, both in conditions of work and pay, made large areas of factory life more attractive than some other occupations. Yet without passing carelessly over a problem that is still very real—especially in the monotony that accompanies mechanised labour, however, "improved" its conditions may be—I must contend that the essential personal problem of winning through monotonous occupations is by no means peculiar to the industrial and manual worker. I recall my first incursion into a world of business which had greatly stimulated boyish ambitions. After an apprenticeship in office boy's chores I rejoiced in a junior clerkship in the South Staffordshire Water Works Company. My first task was to write out demand notes for water rates in the district of Kingswinford. I have never seen Kingswinford but it is more real to me than Troy. I can recall the names of its streets and the feckless inhabitants who never paid their rates until I had written a Second and then a Final Application. I can feel the surface of the paper of those demand notes as I wore out innumerable pennibs on them. I can smell the fresh bundles of them as I cut their wrappings. And most of all I can recall my emotion when, having toiled for weeks on the first set of quarterly demands, doing nothing but write names, addresses and figures for seven hours a day, I reported to the chief clerk and naïvely expected a change of occupation.

"What do I do next, Sir?" I asked.

"Start on the next Quarter's," was the gruff reply. In due course I managed to "improve my position" and gained what was then regarded in my circles as an enviable post —a clerkship in the Birmingham City Treasurer's Department. But all that happened in the first twelve months was that in place of demand notes I wrote out cheques—book after book of them ("But never, oh never, a one for me") with the added strain that whereas a mechanical slip on a demand note could be remedied with the waste-paper basket, an alteration on a cheque required the initial of the City Treasurer and a carpet interview with the exalted one.

These are trivial recollections but there is a meaning in them. In all the vocational changes through which I have since passed, life has never let me off the demand-note discipline, so to speak. For better or for worse Kingswinford is another "city in the soul". After the

City Treasurer's Department came the Army and route marches—

Boots, boots, boots, boots—

with a life more fundamentally uncongenial than I have ever known. A complete transformation came with the turning point that led to the ministry, but it brought a discipline of study that has never been easy and at no point since has it been possible to dissociate what I have known to be real vocational fulfilment from the most persistent necessity for "getting down to it" or "sticking it", at a point where nature has rebelled against monotony and, so far as the senses are concerned, I have been condemned to uncongenial employment. I am convinced that vocational peace in any sphere involves coming to terms with life's chores whether demanded of us by the larger operations of society or arising from the nature of all creative work, especially in that supreme creative calling of home and family life. And it seems to me that the secret of achievement (which is more than endurance) is twofold. It lies partly in Vision—in that imaginative recognition of the place which ten thousand trivial operations have in the total well-being of society and of God's purpose for it. And it depends again on Integrity, on pride in doing a trivial job to perfection and thus to the Glory of God.

When to these considerations there is added the fact that more and more, from the Christian standpoint, life's significance is seen to turn on personal relationships and that the supreme arena within which we are to fulfil the most mighty purpose of all is wherever two or three are met together, it will be understood that I regard "true joy in life" as being within reach of the many rather than the vocational privilege of the few. I say this without, I hope, any blunting of sensibility towards those whose circumstances make it hard for them to experience this. Indeed, it is this last consideration—the realization that so many people are unfulfilled in the use which life makes of them, whether through faults of circumstance, insight or character, that introduces into this question of "being used" by a "mighty purpose" something central and peculiar to *Christian* vocation. To this I now turn.

There is a difference between that vocational adjustment to life which can make us at home in almost any circumstances and tasks, and the consciousness of a calling which takes charge of circumstances, compels us to the development and use of particular gifts and fashions for us a particular way of life. Apart from its special accent in Christian vocation, this calling-out of men and women by life's mighty purposes is a fairly common experience. It may determine the choice of professions and occupations: it lies at the core of all creative work in the arts and in the pursuit of the sciences. Incidentally, it involves acceptance of a very personal responsibility for mastering circumstances, for taking initiatives and summoning courage to overcome; and it does all this even when it provides no way of escape from the discipline of chores. In regard to all this I would only say that spiritual peace can never be won or received if we ignore these vocational compulsions and decline the effort, discipline and responsibility of "being used". This is different from saying that we must all "succeed" vocationally in order to be at peace. Success and recognition are secondary and they may be dependent on circumstances which for the time being cannot be sufficiently changed. Not success but obedience is the determining point in vocational fulfilment. If we know we are "called" to the use of certain gifts, to the acquisition or development of certain faculties, there is no spiritual peace to be found in refusing the call—and putting the blame on circumstance.

The supremely distinctive feature in Christian vocation operates on our minds and consciences in much the same way as the compulsions to which I have just referred. It may also include awareness of particular gifts which will find maximum expression through certain professions and callings. But it has to do less with gifts than with purpose, with God's central disclosure of Himself in Christ. From our perception of this central fact in the Christian revelation there proceed four characteristic features of Christian vocation.

The first is that impulse to worship and glorify God by the integrity of our service, of which I have already written in this and the preceding chapter. The second is the necessity to proclaim and bear witness—to make known the fact of Christ and His saving Gospel, articulating it in word as well as in life. The third is the obligation to care—to care, "for Christ's sake", for all sorts and conditions of men. "The love of Christ constraineth us . . . that they which live should not henceforth live unto themselves." The fourth is the apostolic or missionary element in vocation. This is akin to the witnessing and the caring but it carries with it a peculiar depth of obligation to go forth in the Name. It does this both in the geographical sense of going into all the world with the saving news, and in the deeper sense of thrusting across all frontiers beyond which there lies an unredeemed situation; crossing the cultural, social, political and economic frontiers between the Kingdom of God and "the world".

Now in essence something of all these four obligations or "constraints" belongs to the vocation of every Christian man and woman. Whatever our means of livelihood, our trade or profession, it is possible and necessary that life should be lived within this fourfold calling of worship, witness, caring and evangelizing. Difference in circumstances, aptitude and gifts will result in varying ways of responding to the call, but the common chord of discipleship lies here.

It is out of this universal Christian obligation—a "priesthood of all believers"—that there emerge the specialized vocations of the Christian Church. Out of the general vocation to worship there comes to some a decisive setting-apart for those ministries of the Church which both express the universal summons and provide for men's response to it. From all the witness-bearers some are called and endowed for the task of proclamation through prophetic utterance of the Word. Again, the caring obligation and privilege of the many becomes the specialized pastoral vocation of the "cure of souls". And the apostolic obligation of all thrusts out some into ministries which testify, with peculiar challenge and power, to a Gospel which seeks and saves and a Church which reaches out to the ends of the earth.

It has been my very great privilege to know both the general and special vocations which I have here described. That I have, therefore, been given opportunities and means of grace which have contributed to my own spiritual nurture as well as constituted a way of obedience I can only acknowledge with gratitude. I would, however, add that for me neither perception nor fulfilment of my call have set me free from the necessity to walk but a step at a time, discovering the next "leading" by exercising such powers of discrimination as I can command, weighing up circumstances and learning the larger significance of my call by obedience in an immediate situation. As I have already testified, the sense of being used by a mighty purpose has provided continuity between the general and special stages of my vocational experience. From this has proceeded that "true joy in life" which has been one of Faith's greatest gifts to me. But just as it has provided no exemption from the discipline of chores, so it has not allowed me to escape from the recurrent necessity of coping with a new situation in which, even within the context of my central vocation, discernment and obedience have been costly processes. In my experience the called life is not the placid one, however strong may be its central note of certainty. Freedom to disobey remains with us, with its infinite possibilities for good and ill. When I have shirked I have realized by what easy steps life could become purposeless and its true joy lost. As I have obeyed, insight has been clarified, capacity for service enlarged, and even for me there has been proved again the truth that "all things work together for good to them that love God, to them who are the called according to His purpose".

CHAPTER SIX

FREEDOM FROM THE WORST

"TRUE peace arises from knowing the worst first, and then our freedom from it," wrote Richard Sibbes* in the seventeenth century. By "freedom from it" Sibbes was not thinking of any exemption from "the slings and arrows of outrageous fortune". He was writing with conviction that *amidst* the worst and even while encountering an excessive share of misfortunes and "disquietments", the Christian could possess a deep serenity of mind and enjoy great freedom of spirit.

How bad "the worst" can be we know probably better than did Richard Sibbes. At this point I am not going to offer any further description or analysis of the *malaise* of our time or enlarge upon its sombre disclosures of what human nature is capable of. My concern in this chapter is to testify that even if the age be darker than hitherto and the grounds for fear more serious than we once thought, true peace and spiritual freedom are as accessible to the Christian man as they have ever been.

While writing with an eye upon the stormy happenings of his time—civil war threatening in the Commonwealth and schism in the Church—it is significant that Sibbes called his treatise on spiritual peace "The Soul's Conflict *with Itself*". Although I believe that our uneasiness today is genuinely due, more than hitherto, to concern about the state of the times and events which the average indi-

* A puritan divine whose devotional writings exercised a very wide influence. Francis Quarles and Izaak Walton acknowledge their spiritual indebtedness to him. The quotation is from '*The Soul's Conflict with Itself*'. *A Treatise of the Inward disquietments of distressed spirits, with comfortable remedies to establish them.*

vidual is apparently powerless to influence, I am none the less certain that the most fruitful source of personal anxiety and spiritual stress lies nearer to hand than Moscow or Lake Success, Palestine or Hyderabad, or even the atomic bomb stock-piles and the bacteriological warfare laboratories. I stress this in the interests of honest testimony as well as true diagnosis. I think I am fairly sensitive to the pressure upon all our spirits of the large-scale sorrows through which we have passed and the burden which the corporate problems and dilemmas of our time lay upon our hearts. I nevertheless, know that from day to day and hour to hour my inward peace and personal wholeness are subject to much more immediate influences than are generated by the most sensitive and conscientious response to the state of the world in general. The wrong sort of head at breakfast-time can weigh more than the grave judgments of a *Times* leader: it can, indeed, secure that the leader and the news shall go unread. More seriously, the death of one person near and dear to us touches our soul's condition far more powerfully than the most sympathetic reading of a distant disaster involving the deaths of thousands. Our sympathetic awareness of the significance of the distant and (to us) less personal event ought usually to be deeper than it is. We can—and ought—to grow in this capacity for sympathetic attention. But the fact which I have just stated remains, and it belongs to the nature of things. Indeed, it is from this source that the deepening and widening of our sympathies can best proceed.

I have illustrated my contention by asserting a familiar truth—that what are literally life-and-death affairs (as in news of a bereavement) touch our spirits with a potency proportionate to their personal and inward relationship to us. I will return later to the problem of coping with the spiritual burden which the needs of the world in general constitute for our enlarging sympathies. Here I stress again the truth that our personal wholeness of spirit is subject most immediately to weaknesses and fears which operate from within rather than from without. It is here that we inevitably know "the worst first", and if we are to be whole enough to deal with a wider and larger "worst", we need to receive "our freedom from" this worst within.

One of the earliest and most persistent inward threats to our spiritual poise is fear of disappointment. It is a childish trait but one which accounts for recurrent moods of childishness through our adult life. Its power is not only prolonged through the years; it also goes deep and may corrode our central beliefs. The source of a good many cynical "convictions", as well as the origin of bitter streaks and twists in character, often lies in a personal disappointment which we have been unable to deal with effectively. To a greater or lesser extent (though in us all a considerable one) we crave the good opinion of men and fear to fall short of it or be slighted. At least to the same extent we are ambitious and fear failure or mediocrity. Our natural opinion of ourselves causes us to expect from a just universe a certain amount of recognition or a reasonable share of life's rewards, and we fear that in these things injustice may be our lot. Even the fears that are by no means merely selfish—concern for loved ones and dread of bereavement—nevertheless include a large element of mistrust in our own capacity to endure hurt and loss at a depth where the well-being of one is inextricably bound up with that of another. "I don't know what I should do if . . ." "I couldn't bear it." Familiar phrases of this kind are an admission of limited inward resources and fear of being tested beyond them. True peace arises from knowing the worst first concerning this inner frailty of ours—and then our freedom from it.

I suppose my life has been a "fortunate" one. Certainly it has afforded me blessings which leave me with a sense of immeasurable indebtedness. Addison's joyous hymn speaks of—as well as to—my condition:

> *Ten thousand thousand precious gifts*
> *My daily thanks employ,*
> *Nor is the least a cheerful heart*
> *That tastes those gifts with joy.*

If this book were even more an autobiography than it has been in danger of becoming I would call it *General Thanksgiving*. And yet I am bound to say that my experiences of disappointment and of inward misgiving have been legion and they show little sign of abating. I am not going to take up space to wallow in the recollection or narration of them. My testimony is more concerned with remedies than ailments. I will only add that I have long since discovered that there can be no immunity from assaults of this kind. We can learn how to deal with them but we can be given no assurance that the encounter will not be renewed. Indeed, one factor in achieving peace of mind in relation to them is to accept the fact that they are certain to come again—and find us ready to meet them.

Christian security against this inner fearfulness operates —so I have found—in two ways. It compels attention to a centre of reference outside ourselves, and it makes accessible to us spiritual energies which are more than a match for any new demand. Release from self-centredness is the starting point towards this freedom of spirit. There is a story (I am not sure of its source) of a young enquirer who sought a remedy for anxiety and light on his problems from a certain Indian *Sadhu*. After learning the purpose of the visit the Indian said:

"Problems? Thou hast acquired the Western habit of worrying and running the universe. Whose universe is it, thine or Brahma's?"

It makes a profound difference, not least in terms of moral obedience and responsibility for action, whether we here accept the name "Brahma" or read "the God and Father of our Lord Jesus Christ", but in its sharp deflecting of a personal anxiety from the anxious human self to the real centre of the universe, here is authentic spiritual guidance. In the *Apocalypse of Esdras* there is a similar lifting of a personal burden—this time one that arises from anxiety over others—to the point where it primarily belongs:

"Thou art sore troubled in mind for Israel's sake. Lovest thou that people more than he that made them?"*

This emphasis does not mean that we should care less, but it does demand that we should pay more attention to the source and fulfilment of all true caring and not imagine even in our least selfish and more Christian concerns, that we have become pivotal to the universe.

It is this same deflection of attention from self to God that enables us to put personal disappointment and the fear of it in its proper place. Again and again, as I have said to myself "Whose universe is it, thine or God's?" I have found it possible to look with new detachment upon my own concerns, my inner hopes and fears and all life's little rebuffs and frettings, and I think I have been able to do so without weakening my sense of personal responsibility. Often it has been possible to laugh at the nature of the anxiety or the silly pride which magnified it. Nearly always I have then seen how to learn from the experience and to make disappointment or failure the occasion for

* II Esdras, v. 33.

a new and better beginning. Not least important, I believe it has enabled me to think differently about other people who are clearly at the mercy of their disappointments, so that, without taking them too seriously, a little more thoughtful wisdom and wholesome sympathy have been available for dealing with them.

This shifting of the centre of the problem from self to the Self of the universe leads to that second Christian safeguard against inner frailty—reliance on spiritual energies outside ourselves. This, of course, underlies the whole testimony of this book and I shall have occasion to refer still further to it, at a point of deeper need than that which I am now discussing. The fact to which I would here testify is my profound and vivid sense of the imminence of spiritual forces upon which, by simple, direct action, we can cast our personal weakness and find it remedied. This is inseparable from what I have said previously about putting to the test, in personal attitude and committal, the Christian faith that God is personal. But in description of the experience as well as in doctrinal affirmation about it, I find it most natural to speak about Spirit—the Holy Spirit—as well as about God the Father.

A critical point in my own apprehension of this mystery came after a prolonged period of strain in which my Christian obedience was clearly proving much more of a burden than a freedom. Though more in earnest about Christian discipleship than I had ever been before I seemed further than ever from possessing, even in anticipation, "the glorious liberty of children of God". Nights were wakeful with anxiety and days were tired with it. At last it dawned on me ("dawn" is the right association) that this way of fretful living was a complete negation of the Faith from which my Christian obligation sprang, and that if I honestly meant business about obedience I could really depend upon an encompassing Spirit to deal both with weakness and fear. At that point Christian fidelity came to mean for me not one more frantic effort to achieve the impossible, but a new relaxing of the tension and confident reliance upon a Spirit through which all things are possible.

I know that there is nothing very original about this testimony. But to discover this familiar truth vindicated for oneself in a simple act of personal reliance becomes a stirringly original experience. The lesson may have to be relearned, as I have found, for so many of the prevailing assumptions and characteristics of our time—even within the life of the Church and amidst the outward dispensations of grace—make it all too easy to lose this final simplicity of reliance upon the fact of the Spirit. But—to borrow the language of Richard Sibbes again—I know no more "comfortable remedy" than this for dealing with the "disquietments" which I have been discussing.

As to the "how" of this remedy, I can only point to the oft-described ways by which our spirits most naturally acknowledge their reliance on the Spirit of God. At the particular personal crisis which I have recalled, the liberating rebuke came to me as I lay in bed, weary of the night. I did not then kneel in prayer, or consult Scripture. I merely and literally turned over into a new position of rest, breathed a sigh of relief, felt something like laughter within, and sank into a deep and peaceful sleep from which I woke with a new readiness for the day's responsibilities. Figuratively, if less literally, this attitude has since been a characteristic part of my prayer life, both in private and within the fellowship of the Church. It is bound up with that submissive element in worship of which I have spoken in a previous chapter, and it becomes part of the receptivity with which I respond to that most tender of all liturgical invitations to "take this holy Sacrament to your comfort".

There are deeper levels than those which I have so far touched upon at which true peace is dependent on knowing a graver "worst" and being assured of our freedom from it. One of these is at the point where we meet in human nature something more terrifying than fear of disappointment or a sense of fraility and insufficiency. The other is where we are confronted with happenings in the world about us which awaken the awful misgiving that

> *The pillared firmament is rottenness,*
> *And earth's base built on stubble.*

These several needs run into one another and they cannot in experience be dealt with separately, for the essential remedy of them all is one and indivisible. Yet the two great needs which I have just instanced call for particular recognition. Both of these raise issues which it would be an impertinence to pretend to deal with in a few pages or on the basis of a single personal experience only; yet as this book is primarily personal testimony I offer my own comment, not as "dealing with" the issues but bearing my witness to the way in which the Christian Faith has taught me—and is still teaching me—to think of these matters.

The Christian doctrine of man—man as seen within the potentialities of the Gospel—carries with it the assurance that mankind can reach, in the power of the Spirit, immeasurable heights of moral achievement. Christian history carries its own evidence of this assurance in an apostolic succession of goodness and in the moral transformations which have accompanied a missionary Evangel. If this accent is lost in the preaching of the Gospel it ceases to be Good News in the full significance of New Testament Christianity. And yet, there is another accent in the Gospel which is no less fundamental. Indeed, if we miss it we are likely to miss the real dynamic of the Faith and to find the high hopes which the Good News encourages falsified. This other emphasis is the frank recognition —franker and, in a sense, more pessimistic than is any non-Christian doctrine of man—of the appalling possibilities of human nature apart from God. Only in honest acceptance of this abysmal "worst" in man, and in an utterly humble attitude of mind concerning it, is there any hope of finding freedom from it through the spiritual dynamic of the Gospel.

As I have already acknowledged in the beginning of this chapter, none of us who have lived through recent years can be left in any doubt about the sinister possibilities of human nature. We have been alive in the era of Buchenwald. Yet merely to be aware of this as an awful fact external to ourselves and somehow to hold on to the possibility that one of these days, through the patience and goodness of God, history will have a better tale to tell concerning mankind in general, is not to apprehend the Christian doctrine of redemption or to touch its saving dynamic. One of the most dangerous heresies in discussing this matter is to treat it in the third person and to generalize about mankind's need and God's grace. All that I have just said about "mankind" and "human nature" has to be re-written in the first person and the frightening significance of the worst acknowledged from within. I am very sensitive to the danger of unreality in a discussion of this sort. If we move from utter sincerity in such a matter all our argument about it becomes spiritually dead. I am not posing as a Buchenwald guard or pretending that our differences in moral attainment are a mere façade. Yet I have known full well during these last years how easily the mind—any mind, *my* mind—feeds on

horror and reacts to it. One of the most disturbing features of Buchenwald pictures was the way in which,
being nauseated by them, something within me wanted to
see more. At least I recognized the psychological genius
which trained originally "decent" men to do these things
by setting them down amidst the cruelty and the filth and
letting decent but susceptible minds be influenced by it.
But without dwelling further on this dark spot, I must
confess that another of the frightening realizations of these
last years has been to experience in myself as well as discern in others a progressive hardening of heart against
"undue" sensitiveness. Policies and practices which were
once "unthinkable" so soon become defensible by what
Burke called "the solemn plausibilities of the world".
And the discovery—no, *my* discovery—touches something more intimate than this. With all that richness of
spiritual inheritance and nurture for which I have given
thanks in this book, and that first-hand knowledge of
God's nearness and His Spirit's power which has been
granted to me, I know more today of the dangerous possibilities of my heart than at any time in my life hitherto.
And I more than suspect that, finally, loss of faith in a
beneficent universe is occasioned less by what happens in
the world about us or by the shocking behaviour of other
people; it springs from the final disillusionment that we
cannot trust ourselves and that to try to stand up to the
universe on our own integrity is but "feeling for foothold
through a blank profound".

I will continue this argument in the first person. I think
it is the surest way of keeping my testimony sincere. More
gravely than in earlier days, I "know the worst" (up to
date) about human nature in general and my bit of it in
particular. And yet I can add that I know my "freedom
from it". This is far from being a complacent state of mind

or a confidence which anticipates no further trouble. Eternal vigilance is the condition of this, as of other liberties; or rather, eternal humility and constant reference to God. And here, no language about God and His Fatherly mercy, nor about His Spirit's sustaining power, is adequate without testimony to His saving disclosure of Himself in Christ, crucified and risen.

I will reserve for a closing chapter some endeavour to say a little of what Christ means to me as the key to the rest of my testimony. Here I can only take my place in that centuries' long throng of pilgrims who have come at last to "a place somewhat ascending, and upon that place a cross and a little below, in the bottom, an open sepulchre". Let Bunyan continue the tale:

> "So I saw in my dream that just as Christian came up with the cross, his burden loosed from off his shoulders, and fell from off his back, and began to tumble, and so continued to do till it came to the mouth of the sepulchre, where it fell in, and I saw it no more.
>
> "Then was Christian glad and lightsome, and said with a merry heart: He hath given me rest by his sorrow and life by his death. Then he stood still awhile to look and wonder; for it was very surprising to him that the sight of the cross should thus ease him of his burden. He looked therefore, and looked again, even till the springs that were in his head sent the waters down his cheeks."

I can no more say, in terms which will convince those who have not visited the same place spiritually, *how* this comes to pass than can the thousands before me who have essayed this impossible undertaking. To one man I could read great passages of Paul's *Epistle to the Romans* and say, "Now you understand, don't you?" To another I could offer C. H. Dodd's *Meaning of Paul for Today* or *Commentary on Romans* and say, "That makes it clearer,

doesn't it?" Or I would take someone else to hear the
St. Matthew Passion, and leave it at that. Or I would advise
a friend who has become over-familiar with the New
Testament not to read the Gospels for a few months and
then to try reading aloud and alone the Passion narratives.
Or I would kneel with a friend in prayer. But amidst all
these endeavours I know that the convincing, illuminating
moment would come, not by my efforts and explanations
but through the direct impact of the truth—truth that is
absolute and alive—upon the heart and mind of the
seeker, enabling him at last to say: "I see now, and I
understand why you couldn't explain it better".

After that, we could engage in conversation which
would at least touch the fringe of the how and why. We
could say how we see in the Cross the "type and essence
of all other crosses"; there have been so many and they
keep on being made and used. Yet though Calvary
enhances the poignancy of them all, no other crucifixion
or martyrdom has lifted itself into the same category as the
death of Christ. It has become, through its own inherent
significance, archetypal. We could talk of the curious,
timeless element that gathers round this story. It is a dated
tale, a cruel and unjust execution in the days of Pontius
Pilate. Yet the more one thinks upon it and studies its
historic features, the greater seems the justification for
that contemporary question of the negro spiritual:

> *Were you there when they crucified my Lord?*
> *Sometimes it causes me to tremble.*

If we had a taste for such things we might discuss the
theology of the Atonement. I would have to say how much
of what I have read has hindered rather than helped my
spiritual understanding, and implied a separateness
between God and Christ which is theologically wrong

as well as devotionally hurtful. Yet I should also have to
urge that the word "forgiveness" in the context of the
Cross possesses a depth of meaning which I cannot
ascribe to any other act of forgiveness. I can only speak
of its power as heart-breaking and confess that it is
because of this, more than anything else, that I become
conscious of freedom from the worst that I know about
human nature. And whatever else we tried to say to one
another I should need to say what a bright place Calvary
is for me because always I think of it less as the scene of
the Crucifixion than the Resurrection. It is true that no
place so accentuates the weight of human disobedience
or moves me to a more fearful and responsible recognition of the capacities of my own heart, but somehow I
know the worst here just because the point of revelation
is so very bright. The truth about evil and its remedy
comes home to me in the clean sweet air of a Resurrection
morning. "Glad and lightsome" are the right words.

I wish I were better at the arguments and the reasoning.
But I suspect that if I really had a mind for these things,
I should in the end still be driven to say:

> *Oh could I tell, ye surely would believe it !*
> *Oh could I only say what I have seen !*
> *How should I tell or how can ye receive it,*
> *How, till He bringeth you where I have been?*

But at the heart of this personal awareness of the truth,
the saving perception is that of a God who is revealing,
not hiding Himself; seeking, not eluding search; and even
more eager to reach all men with His gift of freedom from
the worst than we are to be found of Him. To an age
which has more reason than ever to fear the worst, this
news, above all else, needs to be made known to the ends
of the earth.

What I have just written touches the deepest level at

which true peace is our present need. It would, however, be unfair to ignore that quite different reason for misgiving which arises from catastrophic happenings due to other causes than "the worst" in human nature. It is true that what has shaken so many people's faith during these years has been the cruelty of events in which the dark and destructive possibilities of man's heart have been at work. But behind such events as these and apart from the function which freedom-to-choose may play in the scheme of things, there lies the question why goodness and innocence, happiness and peace of mind, should have been left at the mercy of such contingencies as the disasters wrought by evil, the chance bullet and undiscriminating bomb. And this is only one aspect of the wider problem of "contingency"—the accident that, humanly speaking, is unpreventable, the earthquake and flood, the ruined harvest, the premature death.

Again I touch on something which has been the theme of man's most agonizing questions since time began, and to which even the highest reaches of the philosophers and poets have failed to give a final answer in words. This is yet another point at which "true peace" is given by insight rather than reason, though mind and conscience compel continued wrestling with the problem in thought. Once more I offer no more than a personal testimony to the way in which, at this point also, I have accepted the worst and know my freedom from it.

First I would assert in all sincerity that I have habitually reckoned with this worst ever since I began to think about life with any seriousness. In saying this I do not infer that any of us can ignore the problem; but there are ways of thrusting it to the outer margins of thought, or of disguising from ourselves the fact that its bitterness has already made us sceptics at heart, or of narcotizing ourselves by pietistic reliance on a doctrine of "special providence". For me the question raised by this element in life is the sharpest challenge to Christian thought and I remain aware of its sharpness amidst the true peace which has taken from it its bitterness. One reason why it thus holds my attention is that it so frequently and persistently thrusts itself forward not merely in a question posed but in an event happening. Again and again and again, within relationships which make the most powerful claims upon my interest and affection, life's devastating contingency breaks in, and the sharpness of the experience is not abated by its countless repetitions. "He hangeth the earth upon nothing." How can we know "true peace" when any day or hour may bring a fresh and more costly reminder of this precariousness of things? I can only testify that I find it at the place where I also find freedom from the most frightening elements in our human nature—at that Cross which is also the place of Resurrection. That Christ could accept this contingent element in life, become subject to "premature" death, be caught in a chain of events which in their own nature defy rather than fulfil goodness—all this means to me, to begin with (I will put it with a crude simplicity) that we are in good company when these things happen to us. I return here to that timeless and archetypal quality in the Cross which makes Christ's acceptance of it a contemporary fact for us. This sense of being in Christ's company at such moments is not for me an inference, simply. It has become the most certain fact I know about the spiritual life. And though each new experience of catastrophic loss or bereavement tears the flesh again, it becomes at the same time a fresh occasion for discovering how unassailable is the spirit's mastery over the contingencies of time. I am as much at a loss to explain the "how" of this as I am in my other testimony to the power of the Cross. But again I must say how inseparable from this experience is my sense that the Cross, in all its significances, is the place of Resurrection. By this I do not simply mean that it encourages "the blessed hope of immortality" and that I can, therefore, wait in patient anticipation for Eternity's fulfilment of what Time has frustrated. The great truths to which language of this sort points enter into the assurance, of course. But by the Resurrection I mean something much more immediate and contemporary. It is the disclosure of life in its depth, not merely in its post-Time longevity. It is witness to the supremacy of Spirit as the ultimate and unassailable reality. It is evidence of victories eternally secured and of fellowship which no accident can break. In place of dread thoughts about the "finality of death", it convinces me of death's subservience to the living purpose of God—the purpose of that God who (this way of putting it, with all its crudity, expresses something necessary to my testimony) knew what He was doing when He made such a universe our home and destined us, through such spiritual encounters as these, to come into our heritage.

I have necessarily put this in personal terms and I do so with the renewed admission that there remains a final incommunicable element in all such testimony, and this at the point where, for the one testifying, the truth is most real and compelling because of its inwardly convincing power. But crucial as is this sense of personal conviction, I find strength in the realization that what has become so real for me is not a private novelty. It has been characteristic of Christian conviction through the centuries, and in this present age innumerable other men and women have known the truth of it amidst that very "worst" which provokes the sharpest questions. Here I would again say how great and moving has been the evidence for this as

I have met it in recent years through the wider contacts which my work has made possible. I think, for example, of some of the Christian leaders on the Continent of Europe with whom I have taken counsel—men from Norway, Denmark, Holland, Germany and France. I have spoken with men whose personal losses and sufferings make up a tale of immeasurable disaster. Yet it has been to them the most natural thing in the world to make light of it, because in very truth the burden has been light. The total experience has been truly luminous. In the very midst of the darkness—not as a consoling experience afterwards, merely—a spiritual light has shone upon their minds and hearts which has taken away fear, removed all feeling that they were at the mercy of accident and evil, and convinced them that light and goodness and immortality were at that very moment the really victorious factors in the situation. I have met the same testimony at first hand in Chinese and Koreans, and it has been made with the authentic accent of New Testament Christianity, in these present days, by men and women of almost every race. Not least important, nearer home and in many a mean street made shabbier by the "blitz" years, there are folk for whom the realities of a spiritual world which has the Resurrection at the heart of it are a more abiding impression than the devastation which accompanied those years. In the here and now, with more to do in this world and maybe to suffer, they have already tasted immortality. Amidst all the contingencies of Time they have met the worst and found their freedom from it in a present experience of Eternal Life. In the twentieth century they have become "witnesses of the Resurrection and eye-witnesses of His majesty". After that, life can still hurt but it cannot destroy our peace. We have already passed from death to Life.

CHAPTER SEVEN

CONSIDERING THE LILIES

"THINGS high as heaven and deep as hell thou considerest overmuch. Thou dost not consider the lilies sufficiently." John Pulsford gave this advice to seekers after spiritual peace in a less hectic age than this and at a time when the profoundest problems could be solved (or so it now seems to us) with less agony of mind than is involved today. But there is abiding wisdom in this counsel. The quest for Christian certainty needs to include some liberating of attention from fundamental questions and a simple acceptance of present delight in whatsoever things are lovely and of good report. This testimony of mine to the way in which the Faith has kept its hold on me through testing years would be far from complete if it omitted any reference to what the "lilies" have meant for me.

I begin with the sheer content which I have found in very transient loveliness "which today is, and tomorrow . . .". Of course it is just this fleetingness, this fragility of so much that is joyous and beautiful, which constitutes one of life's heart-breaks and for many people is another assault on faith instead of a support to it.

> *The loveliness of Autumn, blue sea and dipping birds,*
> *Harrow and plough, sweet wind and voices,*
> *Accentuate, not still, the trouble of my heart.*

I do not see how I could offer testimony to the power of the "lilies" to renew and refresh the life of my spirit apart from the hold which Christ Himself has on me and the authority which attaches to His words. Dissociated from Himself and read as an argument, His own "If God so clothe the grass . . . shall He not much more clothe you?" is not self-authenticating. It is only when our souls have begun to find their certainty in Him that we can look again at transient beauty and find in it token of everlasting order and care. It is against this background of certainty that I have found so much liberty of spirit in the enjoyment of a thousand-and-one passing delights. I have become less and less anxious about their ephemeral character and more and more able to glory in a present wonder. And I believe the experience has not merely been an escape, least of all an "escape from reality"; it has been renewing and re-creative because these momentary joys are insights into a real and eternal world.

Yet, already, in thus describing the ground of my peace in these experiences, I am departing from what is most characteristic of them. They are not occasions for "taking thought", even thought about "things high as heaven". They are moments of contented, care-free acceptance, asking no questions.

As to the field in which we are most likely to find our lilies, something depends on personal tastes and immediate circumstances. Not many of us are incapable of profiting by a literal acceptance of Christ's advice to consider the lilies. A field of buttercups, Flanders poppies, joy in one's own garden, pride in a window-box (such as those which constituted most of the garden of my earliest home), the restfulness of green meadows and stately lawns, the ripe beauty of harvest fields—in a thousand different forms the most ancient assemblages of fragile beauty meet our gaze. We know they will be gone tomorrow, but in the nature of things to them belongs a second and infinity of advents.

So I went into the field of Ardath and sat among the flowers, and the silver eyes of the field did open unto me and therein I saw signs and wonders.

The occasions have literally been uncountable on which I have drunk grace in moments like these—pottering in my garden, strolling in St. James's Park in a business lunch-hour, looking at flowers in a church (especially when the more voluble articulation of the Word seems to have been off the beauty centre), revelling in colour, form and fragrance. I do most truly feed on these things by faith and with thanksgiving.

Nature has also contributed generously to these delights through some of her more sentient creatures (the comparison does not overlook the sentient character of the lilies), more especially those whose unconscious contributions to the humour of things is a source of such abundant grace. Some of the most blessed of my care-free contemplations in St. James's Park took place during the hardest years of the war. I was only one amongst thousands who took daily refreshment in a saunter there and it was noticeable how many people in authority—political and military—regularly took the same relaxation. I recall one episode on a particularly dark day of the war when I saw a crowd blocking the path by the lakeside. It included various dignitaries in civil and ecclesiastical affairs, with military officers on whom special burdens rested. With my curiosity roused I joined the crowd and was just in time to see what had commanded its attention. A duck, peculiarly quaint in mien, closely followed by a brood of tiny ducklings, was waddling across the path to the water. And the little crowd watched, spell-bound and happy. I know another Lakeside where teaching was offered which gives meaning to things like these.

But, again, it is not meanings I am recording here. It is

acceptances, simply enjoyed. It is enough to add my
spiritual indebtedness to—a family cat who spent three
weeks walking from New Barnet to Walthamstow, across
(presumably) Tottenham and Edmonton, in sure obedience to a homing instinct (more pathos than humour here);
or to another noble-looking and fastidious creature who,
for years, at the sound of tea-time crockery, took up his
position on the arm of a chair and waited for his token
drink (I would go abroad on a ten-thousand mile journey
and return to find him in the same position at the appointed hour). With homage to their Maker I also salute
a succession of mongrels whose blend of cupboard-love
and personal fidelity made them partners in the daily
breaking of bread. Nor should I omit the intriguing ways
of a well-bred Cairn whose lovely eyes, as someone
put it, could tear the heart out of a turnip. In the same
ménage life has also been lightened by an ancient pet rabbit
who has contentedly woffled his nose through the years;
utility value nil; grace value infinite. For ten thousand
moments of pure, foolish joy, brief as the passing laugh
they provoked, yet touched with deeper intimations, I
give thanks. They are inseparable from all life's other
means of grace.

All these pleasures at some point lead into the larger
debt I owe for all aesthetic perceptions and experiences.
It is not within my purpose or competence to discuss the
relation of beauty to truth or of both to revelation and
salvation. That all these things are ultimately one and
indivisible I can have no doubt. Yet I know that beauty
can be pursued without reference to truth in its wholeness
and that it can then become an idolatry that is not merely
formal but spiritually disintegrating. All beauty, for me,
has its source and meaning in God from whom cometh
every good and perfect gift. But no thing of beauty, though

given by God, can say for us, concerning His nature and our obedience what Christ alone has said and revealed. If my soul's peace could be fortified only by His gift of beauty I should remain spiritually unquiet. It is because I have found in Christ God's gift of Himself that I can be most at home in His other gifts of beauty and find peace of spirit there.

But this, again, is speech *about* aesthetic revelation. My testimony is to the joy of perceiving and accepting it, especially to its liberating and re-creative power. Once more I recognize that the fields within which we can most naturally consider these lilies are to be found along paths which differ according to our varying gifts and aptitudes. I will confine my testimony to the one which to me has meant most and in which I think pure aesthetic experience passes into other disclosures of Reality—I mean, the power of music. And because my first introduction to this world of revelation was associated with an act of simple Christian obedience I will venture one more personal recollection and a final tribute to the home in which I learned so much about the beautiful as well as the good.

When I was six or seven it happened that my father learned of a young woman violinist who had become orphaned and was in difficult straits financially. His own precarious condition made it impossible for him to help as generously as he wanted, but he could at least offer without charge the use of our "parlour" where the musician might receive her pupils. Before long the violinist offered in gratitude to give lessons to one of the children and I was the fortunate object of this friendly recompense. Except for the great moments in my direct knowledge of Christ I can recall no experience of a truly revealing character comparable to the effect of the next few years upon my mind and heart. I cannot at this distance assess the

technical competence of this first music teacher of mine.
I think she must have been very gifted; certainly my recollection of her "touch" places her amongst the best musicians I have ever heard. But what I remember best are the
long conversations she had with a wondering youngster
—illustrating them with her instrument—as she talked
about fiddles and musicians and the classical creations for
the violin which were the heritage into which every young
music student could enter. In my most superior moments
since I have never been able to join in disparaging criticism of Mendelssohn for I first heard the whole of his
Violin Concerto (minus the orchestra) as the sole member
of the audience in that parlour above the shop. There, too,
some of the greatest phrases in the Beethoven, Brahms
and Elgar Concertos were quoted in the conversations
between this dear woman's violin and the soul of a child.
Since that time there has scarcely been a week in which
(through the ministrations of others' instruments, not my
own) I have not found liberty of spirit through this gift
of grace.

Music alone could not save me, but its gifts are inseparable from my salvation and there is one respect in
which it continues to illuminate for me the great facts
of our redemption in Christ and to pass from aesthetic
pleasure into a commentary upon the Gospels and an
administration of the Sacraments. This is through the
prophetic and priestly service of John Sebastian Bach, in
his *Church Cantatas*, his *Passions* and the *B Minor Mass*.
With these I inevitably associate Handel's *Messiah* and,
most of all, Elgar's *Dream of Gerontius* whose strains I
expect to hear whenever it becomes time for me to pass
from consciousness of this world to the glories of the life
everlasting. (When mercy has prevailed it will be the
Sanctus of the *B Minor* which I shall be hearing with

my celestial body.) Meantime, few similes better express
my conception of the relation between life in this world
and the next than does the language of John Donne:

> *Since I am coming to that Holy room*
> *Where, with thy Quire of Saints for evermore*
> *I shall be made thy music; as I come*
> *I tune the instrument here at the door,*
> *And what I must do then, think here before.*

Yet again I have mingled with this meditation upon
the lilies, thoughts of "things high as heaven and deep as
hell"; but I bring these deeper types of aesthetic experience within the compass of this chapter because the point
I want specially to emphasize is the way in which their
revealing power operates. It comes, once more, less by
"taking thought" than by relaxation; its chief condition
is simple acceptance. It only requires that we shall turn
to it as to recreation, in the commonest use of the word.
By a care-free yielding of ourselves to its grace we find
it literally a way of re-creation.

This testimony of gratitude for the release which has
followed acceptance of Christ's counsel to consider the
lilies leads me to one other comment. I have spoken of
delight in things ephemeral, in the beauty "which today
is". If these things are to fulfil their ministry there needs
to be brought to them an unstressful readiness to live very
much in the present, taking no thought for the morrow.
We must be content to live a day at a time, even an hour
at a time, a moment at a time.

Now there is, of course, a cynical or sceptical approach
possible to the doctrine of living a day at a time. "Let us
eat, drink and be merry, for tomorrow we die." But there
is also the approach of faith, acceptance of the spiritual
certainty which lay behind Christ's assurance: "Sufficient

unto the day." This does not narcotize our faculties of
recollection or anticipation, nor does it alter the fact that
there is a place for their very responsible exercise within
our total Christian obedience. It does, however, literally
imply that there is no time like the present, and that the
really crucial moment is the immediate now. This is true
of every aesthetic experience; it is of the essence of all
those spirit-liberating insights which the lilies make possible, whether in such fields as I have illustrated or in countless other directions. Of course, recollection also has its
place here, as this testimony of mine confesses. Our immediate delight becomes intensified as we reflect that

> *. . . here I stand, not only with the sense*
> *Of present pleasure, but with pleasing thoughts*
> *That in this moment there is life and food*
> *For future years.*

Yet the joys of recollection and anticipation are *present*
experiences and that which makes a particular moment
worthy of subsequent recollection is its immediate, living
particularity. I know, for example, a great musical work.
I can take pleasure in recollecting moments in which it has
spoken to me in past days. I can think imaginatively of
what new interpretations of it may mean in days to come.
But when, in fact, the hour comes in which I actually hear
anything like a worthy re-presentation of it I say to myself
anew and with precise significance: "Now is the accept-
able time. Now is my soul's peace through music nearer
than when I first believed." There simply is no time like
the present.

At this point I believe the lilies draw our attention to
something that is central to life's meaning and which has
its supreme confirmation in the Christian faith. Even in
relation to things past and future, *now* is the determining

moment. We can stand in such immediate relationship to God, through the power of the Holy Spirit, that His goodness and mercy will redeem the past and His presence assure us that the morrow will take care of itself. Meantime, *now* is the moment for our obedience and for living at that depth which the New Testament calls Eternal Life —the life which is Life indeed. The One who knows all about this "from the other side" points for sign of it to that fleeting manifestation of perfection—a lily. With Him we shift the burden of thoughts high as heaven and deep as hell upon its tender petals, and the burden and the mystery become light.

CHAPTER EIGHT

RISEN TODAY

WHEN Jane Burden first sat for William Morris, the artist spent some time before his canvas and at last showed it to the model. Instead of a picture, the canvas bore the words: "I cannot paint you but I love you." I make no attempt in this chapter to present the picture of Jesus Christ as He appears to me. This is chiefly because I could not do it if I tried; there is no possibility of my making articulate in words the "image" which the name of Jesus brings before my mind and heart. But another consideration is that even if I suceeded in the task it would not be a picture of Christ. It would only be my personal impression of Him, a very partial glimpse of the whole, a slight insight into the full reality of Him. I am not inclined to deal so cavalierly with the works of the masters as was Carlyle, but I can see the point of his outburst when he first saw Holman Hunt's *Light of the World.** After dismissing it as "empty make-believe" (a judgment which I do not share) he said he had seen representations of Jesus by all the greatest artists but "when I look, I say, 'Thank-you, Mr. da Vinci, Thank-you, Mr. Michael Angelo, Thank you, Mr. Raphael, that may be your idea of Jesus Christ, but I've another of my own which I much prefer' ". But Carlyle never produced it.

Although Christ is the centre and soul of my Christian convictions, there is no single picture of Him that I would care to have permanently hanging in my study or bedroom.

* The story is told in William Gaunt's *The Pre-Raphaelite Dream.*

I have learned much from many "Lives" of Him, but there will never be written a "definitive" *Life*. The written sources of all the "Lives"—the Gospels—are unique in the authority with which they present Him, and all our other knowledge of Him has its anchorage there, but even the Gospels are the beginning, not the completion, of what Christian testimony has to say about the "fact of Christ". As the last of the Gospels says in its closing words: "And there are also many other things which Jesus did, the which, if they should be written every one, I suppose that even the world itself could not contain the books that should be written." And we may add that this is true, not only of the "many other things which Jesus did", but of the much else that Jesus is.

This chapter will not, then, contain even an abbreviated "Life of Christ" as I know Him and believe in Him. But I want to add a closing word about the overwhelming pressure on my mind and spirit which is exercised by this Name which is above every name.

All that I have written in this book is part of my testimony to this pressure of the "Fact of Christ". He is the key to my spiritual heritage, whether I think of this in terms of the home through which I first learned His Name and felt His influence, or whether I dwell on the longer and richer inheritance of Christian history. It is because the Bible testifies to Him that I acknowledge in it a peculiar authority for my religious thinking, and yet my understanding of the Bible is more and more determined by the light that He throws upon it. In so far as I can put a meaning to history, it is Jesus who supplies the meaning. My certainty that this historic process has its setting and fulfilment in eternity is related to Him more than to any other source. The life of the Church and my love for it are bound up with Him. My worship has its centre and inspiration in Him. He is inseparable from my experience of Christian fellowship, in the local, visible community of the "gathered" Church, in its world-wide out-reach, and in my consciousness of being at one with the communion of saints. It is from Him that there proceeds that authority before which I find myself constrained to make personal submission, both in obedience to His will and in receptivity towards the gift of His Spirit. He is the explanation of the mighty purpose, in being used by which I find true joy in life. The Cross owes its significance to the fact that it was He who was crucified. The light of the Resurrection is a light that streams from Him. If I can bear to know the worst about the heart of man—my heart —and can feel prepared for the worst that life may do to me, it is because, contemplating these things with Him, I know a freedom of spirit which is sufficient for them. If the mighty convictions, experiences of spiritual certainty, delight in life's graces, and hopes for eternity, of which I have spoken, are all illusory, He is responsible for my being deluded. If—as I am convinced—the final truth about things is better than I have believed or anyone has portrayed, it will be because He is, in fact, the final meaning and truth of the universe.

To speak in such terms as these about Jesus means that I place Him in a category quite different from that occupied, in my thinking, by anyone else who has walked this earth—hero or saint, artist or teacher, lover or friend. And this is not because I believe the "Jesus of history" to have been more wise or heroic, a stauncher friend or one more naturally to be loved, than anyone else. The difference begins at quite another point in thought. It starts with something which has found its way into every chapter of this book and which I can never dissociate from Christian thinking, Christian discipleship, Christian experience or anything else Christian. It is the fact of His Resurrection.

It is relevant here to recall that such records as we have of Christ's life "on earth"—the Gospels—are essentially a product of the Resurrection. This is, in fact, true of the New Testament as a whole. Its earliest contents (for chronologically some of the Epistles are earlier than the Gospels) deal pre-eminently with the "living Christ", while the Gospels themselves, though placing on record the events which preceded the Resurrection, come from pens which are writing in the light and power of it. This is *the* supreme fact about Jesus—that "He could not be holden of death", that nothing which sin or "accident" could do could diminish or terminate the Reality of Him.

At the risk of over-repetition, I must affirm again that the significance of the Resurrection lay in more than its proof that Jesus of Nazareth was immortal. What the Epistles and Gospels testify is not simply that there is a life "after" death. It is that in Jesus there is life in the midst of death, Eternal Life entering into Time, the Life which is of the very essence of God manifesting itself amidst our mortality. It is this which accounts for all those "more than human" characteristics of Him which pervade the Gospel narratives. I speak not only of the "miracles", though I include these. I think even more of the quality of His words. "Never man spake as this man." Part of the tremendous power of the Gospels lies in the "living words" of Jesus which they record. This quality in His words is due to more than their beauty or poetic character; there is a dynamic element in them which accounts, I believe, for the fact that much of what He said could be transcribed long after it was spoken. Some people who heard His words simply could not forget them and they still speak across the centuries with living power.

It is, I think, more true to say, not that they speak across the centuries, but that the quality which was in them when they were first spoken proceeds now from the heart of that Reality which is the living Christ.

This same fact, that the Life which was in Jesus was of the very essence of God—Eternal Life entering into Time —accounts, too, I believe, for his influence on the people who appear in the Gospel records. "Influence" is scarcely a deep enough word to describe His impact upon them. Whether they accepted or rejected Him, this impact was for them of epoch-making significance. Most dramatically it is seen in those who were least whole physically, mentally or psychologically. More significantly it appears in its confronting of men with choices that were to prove of life-and-death importance. They were being met not so much by the challenge of "absolute standards" as by the power of Life as it is in its "absolute" and indestructible nature.

As for the miracles, it may well be that in the course of their transmission the records have received some legendary accretions; I think they have done so; but that the presence of Jesus would result in "mighty works" both in relation to persons and to circumstances, seems to me an inevitable consequence of the fact that the Life which was in Him was to prove greater than death. There is a character in one of William de Morgan's novels (*Joseph Vance*) to whom the author attributes an experience with which most of us have to reckon as we try to assess the significance of this element in the Gospels. de Morgan says of this character:

> "He was a Christian who had endeavoured to strain off the teachings of Jesus the Nazarene from the scum and dregs of the World and the Churches, and had never been able to decide on the mesh of his strainer. . . . He seemed

always to be endeavouring to find a sieve that would let Christ through and keep the miracles out. But do what he would, the Resurrection slipped past. The stone that was rolled away from the sepulchre broke a hole in the mesh and the Gadarene swine found it out and came through with a rush, and then a new sieve had to be provided and the whole operation repeated."

There is a vital difference spiritually between credulity and belief and I do not want to blur the difference. But for me the real issue in this matter is: Does our understanding of Christianity begin with the Resurrection and does this determine our thought concerning the significance of Christ's coming to this world, the nature of His authority, the validity of His teaching, and the possibilities that He opens to us through our Christian obedience? If it does—and I am convinced it should do—then instead of finding in the Gospels much that needs to be "explained away", we find much more that rebukes us for being "fools and slow of heart to believe all that the prophets have spoken", whether in olden times or in more recent days.

This dominating power of the Resurrection in my thought of Jesus has had many consequences. For my purpose in this chapter I speak of two only.

First, it has given to the teaching of Jesus a quality and authority which make it much more than the wisdom of a moralist who could see farther, or who proclaimed higher "ideals", than other experts on conduct. The teaching springs out of the Life. By this, again, I do not simply mean that the conduct of Jesus was consistent with the ideals which he enunciated. The key word once more is Life—which I have to spell with a capital "L". In Him was Life—the very stuff of the universe, the original creative energy that made it, the power that can redeem it when it has gone wrong, the Life of God Himself. What Jesus taught, in the power and wisdom of this Life, was not just a new morality which, judging by the history of mankind hitherto, was no more likely to be practised than the less exacting older moralities. His teaching was a disclosure of the moral and spiritual structure of the universe, and what we often think of as *demands* on conduct are something quite different from demands. They are *directions* as to the way in which our life may be brought under the new power of Life and the essential purpose of the universe fulfilled through us. Christ's warnings against acquisitiveness were not simply ascetic injunctions to do without things; they were reminders of the only way in which we can ever possess the things that really matter. Similarly, that often perplexing but ineradicable element in His teaching and His Life—His warning against trying to resist evil with its own characteristic attitudes and weapons, was not a demand that we should accept defeat and be brave enough or martyr-like enough to go through life unprotected against evil. It was an assurance that real Life—life in fellowship with God—provides better weapons against evil than those which the world normally relies upon. It was a *direction* as to the way of victory. Of course, all this has its consequences for conduct and in the working-out of those consequences sharp problems arise for us, individually and corporately. But by thus associating the teaching of Jesus with the power and authority of His Resurrection, a new quality enters into the business of wrestling with the problems and working out our answers in conduct. We become caught up into the Life— the Life of God—from which the revelation and the teaching proceed.

The second consequence to which I would refer, as following from this dominance of the Resurrection in all my Christian thinking, has to do with its bearing on my conception of the character of God. In earlier chapters I have said much about my trust in a personal God and how I believe such trust to be demanded by the biblical view of life.

Whenever, by deep inward committal, I have put to the test this faith in a personal God, the Faith has held me with a convincing power which has made my dealings with God—or rather, His dealings with me—the supreme personal transactions of my life. What I must here add is that although I find in the Bible, as a whole, compelling justification for putting my trust in God as a Person, it is the Risen Christ alone who enables me to discern something of the lineaments of that Person. I have already indicated my acceptance of the Church's view (portrayed in its doctrine of the Trinity) that the ultimate truth about the nature of the Godhead is a mystery that is only apprehended aright as we think of God the Father and God the Holy Spirit as well as God the Son. At this point we have to confess that insight goes beyond speech and that our doctrines are but adumbrations, not definitions, of the final mysteries. But once again, the luminous centre of the mystery—that which reveals the Fatherhood and the way of the Spirit—is the fact of Jesus Christ, Risen. In Him I come as near to seeing the Face of God as mortal man can ever do in this world, and I believe it will be in Him that I see whatever more of that Face will be granted me to see in the next. And there is one quality in it which moves me to wonder, love and praise more than anything else. It is that quality which made it natural for Jesus on earth to say, at a moment when He was more explicit about the mystery of His relationship to the Father than at any other time: "Come unto me, all ye that labour and are heavy laden and I will give you rest. Take my yoke upon you and learn of me, for I am meek and lowly in heart, and ye shall find rest unto your souls."

For I am meek and lowly in heart. Like Father, like Son. On the throne of this universe—author of its beauty, master of its secrets, wielder of its powers—a humble-minded God.

Is that why so many of us fail to see Him and to find rest to our souls?